POETRY *alive*

REFLECTIONS

South Central Interior Distance
Education School

Box 4700 Stn Main Merritt BC V1K 1B8
250 378 4245 or 1 800 663 3536

POETRY *alive*

REFLECTIONS

COMPILED AND EDITED BY

Larry Liffiton
and
John McAllister
Calgary Board of Education

SERIES EDITOR

Dom Saliani
Calgary Board of Education

Copp Clark Pitman Ltd.
A Longman Company
Toronto

Pearson Education Canada Inc.

Any request for photocopying, recording, taping, or for storing on information storage and retrieval systems of any part of this book shall be directed in writing to the Canadian Reprography Collective, 214 King Street West, Suite 312, Toronto, Ontario M5H 3S6.

ISBN 0-7730-5167-8

EDITING: Muriel Fiona Napier
DESIGN: Jo-Anne Slauenwhite
COVER DESIGN AND ILLUSTRATION: Sharon Matthews
ART DIRECTION: Kyle Gell
TEXT ILLUSTRATIONS: Kyle Gell, Steve MacEachern, Allan Moon
TYPESETTING: Marnie Morrissey
PRINTING AND BINDING: The Bryant Press Limited

Acknowledgment
We should like to thank our families, especially our wives, Susan and Lauri, for their support, advice, and tolerance throughout this project.

Canadian Cataloguing in Publication Data

Main entry under title:

Reflections

(Poetry alive)
Includes index.
ISBN 0-7730-5167-8

1. English poetry.   2. American poetry.
3. Canadian poetry (English).*   I. Liffiton, Larry.
II. McAllister, John, 1951–   III. Series.
PN6101.R44 1993   821.008   C92-093385-8

Printed and bound in Canada

5 6 7 8 - GG - 02 01

# POETRY

MARIANNE MOORE

I, too, dislike it: there are things that are important beyond all this
        fiddle.
    Reading it, however, with a perfect contempt for it, one discovers in
    it after all, a place for the genuine.
        Hands that can grasp, eyes
        that can dilate, hair that can rise
            if it must, these things are important not because a

high-sounding interpretation can be put upon them but because they
        are
    useful. When they become so derivative as to become unintelligible,
    the same thing may be said for all of us, that we
        do not admire what
        we cannot understand: the bat
            holding on upside down or in quest of something to

eat, elephants pushing, a wild horse taking a roll, a tireless wolf under
    a tree, the immovable critic twitching his skin like a horse that feels a
        flea, the base-
    ball fan, the statistician—
        nor is it valid
            to discriminate against "business documents and

school-books"; all these phenomena are important. One must make a
        distinction
    however: when dragged into prominence by half poets, the result
        is not poetry,
    nor till the poets among us can be
        "literalists of
        the imagination"—above
            insolence and triviality and can present

for inspection, "imaginary gardens with real toads in them," shall
        we have
    it. In the meantime, if you demand on the one hand
    the raw material of poetry in
        all its rawness and
        that which is on the other hand
            genuine, you are interested in poetry.

ƤOETRY: *REFLECTIONS OF LIFE*

A poet distils the essence of personal experience into words that reflect the wide scope and variety of adventures we all encounter on the journey of life. The poems in this anthology capture those reflections.

Life's journey begins with much eagerness and a hunger to discover what the future holds. As the direction of the road unfolds, much of what is "childlike" is lost as the emerging adult takes shape. The journey can become a solitary one; sometimes by choice, sometimes by circumstance. At other times, crossroads bring crowded highways and close travelling companions. Farewells are inevitable as we each choose different paths or reach journey's end.

The crossroads we encounter on our road through life often invite us to pause for a moment and reflect on what we see, or where we are. Some of our reflections might raise doubts about the nature of the journey, creating the impression that we are travelling in the dark. Questions concerning the nature and integrity of people might also arise provoking criticism and a call for change. New avenues will be forged in the evolution of relationships between women and men. If life at times seems too complex and overwhelming, refuge can be sought in the simplicity and peace of a greener, more natural world. As the journey draws to a close, our reflections of life become a legacy for the next generation of travellers.

CONTENTS

1 THE HUNGRY HEART

2 THE CHILD I WAS

vii

3 A STRANGER NOW

4 THE HUMAN TOUCH

5 ⟨THE LAST JOURNEY

6 BROKEN IMAGES

7 PLAYING THE FOOL

8 STILL SEPARATE IDENTITIES

9 GREENER GRASS

10 THE LEGACY

ACTIVITIES

ESSAYS

1 THE HUNGRY HEART

1

THE POEMS

2

I HAVE ALWAYS KNOWN

NARIHIRA
(Trans. Kenneth Rexroth)

I have always known
That at last I would
Take this road, but yesterday
I did not know that it would be today.

*T*HE ROAD NOT TAKEN

ROBERT FROST

Two roads diverged in a yellow wood,
And sorry I could not travel both
And be one traveler, long I stood
And looked down one as far as I could
To where it bent in the undergrowth;

Then took the other, as just as fair,
And having perhaps the better claim,
Because it was grassy and wanted wear;
Though as for that the passing there
Had worn them really about the same,

And both that morning equally lay
In leaves no step had trodden black.
Oh, I kept the first for another day!
Yet knowing how way leads on to way,
I doubted if I should ever come back.

I shall be telling this with a sigh
Somewhere ages and ages hence:
Two roads diverged in a wood, and I—
I took the one less traveled by,
And that has made all the difference.

${\mathcal S}$HOOTING THE SUN

AMY LOWELL

Four horizons cozen me
To distances I dimly see.

Four paths beckon me to stray,
Each a bold and separate way.

Monday morning shows the East
Satisfying as a feast.

Tuesday I will none of it,
West alone holds benefit.

Later in the week 'tis due
North that I would hurry to.

While on other days I find
To the South content of mind.

So I start, but never rest
North or South or East or West.

Each horizon has its claim
Solace to a different aim.

Four-souled like the wind am I,
Voyaging an endless sky,
Undergoing destiny.

4

THE ORANGE

RAYMOND SOUSTER

Each new week is a shiny orange
which you divide into seven portions,
making it come out as even as you can.

Then each morning comes that glorious moment
when you carefully lift one piece to your waiting mouth,
feel your teeth ripping deep through the pulpy fruit
to release golden jets that flood and tingle
all the long way down your suddenly-pulsing throat.

THE BUS

LEONARD COHEN

I was the last passenger of the day,
I was alone on the bus,
I was glad they were spending all that money
just getting me up Eighth Avenue.
Driver! I shouted, it's you and me tonight,
let's run away from this big city
to a smaller city more suitable to the heart,
let's drive past the swimming pools of Miami Beach,
you in the driver's seat, me several seats back,
but in the racial cities we'll change places
so as to show how well you've done up North,
and let us find ourselves some tiny American fishing village
in unknown Florida
and park right at the edge of the sand,
a huge bus pointing out,
metallic, painted, solitary,
with New York plates.

DVENTURE

ELISE MACLAY

"Like a good many people who are in or above their seventies, Mother had far more courage and curiosity than fear."

I read that in a book recently and I thought, it's true. While I'm still too afraid too often, I've shed a lot of my fears. I worry less. I used to think this or that action could affect my whole life. Well, most of my life is behind me now, and what's ahead probably won't be worth sacrificing current adventure for.

Like the man said. "Do you want to live forever?"

I don't know about that; I do know I want to live for real. So when I hesitate, I tell myself: You have hardly anything to lose.

So open the door. Ask the question. Accept the invitation.

Get on the bus. Try it. Go alone.

Climb. Plunge. Explore.

$\mathcal{P}$RAXIS

SHARON THESEN

Unable to imagine a future,
imagine a future better
than now, us creatures
weeping *in the abattoir*
only make noise & do
not transform a single fact.
So stop crying. Get up. Go out. Leap
the mossy garden wall
the steel fence or whatever
the case may be & crash
through painted arcadias,
fragments of bliss & roses
decorating your fists.

$\mathcal{F}$OR THE YOUNG WHO WANT TO

MARGE PIERCY

Talent is what they say
you have after the novel
is published and favorably
reviewed. Beforehand what
you have is a tedious
delusion, a hobby like knitting.

Work is what you have done
after the play is produced
and the audience claps.
Before that friends keep asking
when you are planning to go
out and get a job.

Genius is what they know you
had after the third volume
of remarkable poems. Earlier
they accuse you of withdrawing,
ask why you don't have a baby,
call you a bum.

The reason people want M.F.A.'s,
take workshops with fancy names
when all you can really
learn is a few techniques,
typing instructions and some-
body else's mannerisms

is that every artist lacks
a license to hang on the wall
like your optician, your vet
proving you may be a clumsy sadist
whose fillings fall into the stew
but you're certified a dentist.

The real writer is one
who really writes. Talent
is an invention like phlogiston
after the fact of fire.
Work is its own cure. You have to
like it better than being loved.

THE PETALS OF THE TULIPS

JUDITH HEMSCHEMEYER

The petals of the tulips
just before they open

when they're pulling
the last dark purple energy through the stem

are covered with a whitish veil,
a caul.

I like them best then:

they're me the month before I was born

the month Mother spent
flat on her back in the hospital.

The way I found out—

once, in round eight of one of our fights
I hissed at her, "I didn't ask to be born!"

and she threw back her head and howled,
remembering,

"You? You?

Hot as it was that summer
I had to lie there for weeks
hanging on to you.

You? You were begging to be born!"

from GIRL'S-EYE VIEW OF RELATIVES

PHYLLIS McGINLEY

FIRST LESSON

The thing to remember about fathers is, they're men.
A girl has to keep it in mind.
They are dragon-seekers, bent on improbable rescues.
Scratch any father, you find
Someone chock-full of qualms and romantic terrors,
Believing change is a threat—
Like your first shoes with heels on, like your first bicycle
It took such months to get.

Walk in strange woods, they warn you about the snakes
    there.
Climb, and they fear you'll fall.
Books, angular boys, or swimming in deep water—
Fathers mistrust them all.
Men are the worriers. It is difficult for them
To learn what they must learn:
How you have a journey to take and very likely,
For a while, will not return.

SHE'S LEAVING HOME

JOHN LENNON AND PAUL McCARTNEY

Wednesday morning at five o'clock as the day begins,
Silently closing her bedroom door,
Leaving the note that she hoped would say more,
She goes downstairs to the kitchen
Clutching her handkerchief,
Quietly, turning the backdoor key,
Stepping outside she is free.
          She (We gave her most of our lives.)
          is leaving (Sacrificed most of our lives.)
          home. (We gave her everything money could buy.)
She's leaving home after living alone
For so many years.

Father snores as his wife gets into her dressing gown,
Picks up the letter that's lying there.
Standing alone at the top of the stairs,
She breaks down and cries to her husband,
"Daddy, our baby's gone.
Why would she treat us so thoughtlessly?
How could she do this to me?"
          She (We never thought of ourselves.)
          is leaving (Never a thought for ourselves.)
          home. (We struggled hard all our lives to get by.)
She's leaving home after living alone
For so many years.

Friday morning at nine o'clock she is far away,
Waiting to keep the appointment she made,
Meeting a man from the motor trade.
          She (What did we do that was wrong?)
          is having (We didn't know it was wrong.)
          fun. (Fun is the one thing that money can't buy.)
Something inside that was always denied
For so many years.
She's leaving home. Bye, Bye.

ℱATHER AND SON

CAT STEVENS

F It's not time to make a change, just relax
take it easy, you're still young that's your
fault there's so much you have to know. Find
a girl settle down. If you want you can marry,
look at me, I'm old but I'm happy.
I was once like you are now, and I know that
it's not easy to be calm when you've found
something going on, but take your time, think
a lot, why think of everything you've got.
For you will still be here tomorrow but your
dreams may not.
S How can I try to explain, 'cause when I do
he turns away again. It's always been the same
same old story. From the moment I could talk
I was ordered to listen, now there's a way and
I know that I have to go. Away, I know, I have
to go.

F It's not time
to make a change,
just sit down take
it slowly, you're
still young that's

S Away away away,
I know I have to
make this decision
alone—no.

your fault, there's so much you have to go
through. Find a girl settle down if you want
you can marry, look at me, I am old but I'm
happy.

S All the times
that I've cried
keeping all the
things I knew inside
it's hard, but it's

F Stay stay stay,
why must you go and
make this decision
alone?

harder to ignore it. If they were right I'd agree
but it's them they know not me now there's a
way and I know that I have to go away, I know
I have to go.

ULYSSES

ALFRED, LORD TENNYSON

It little profits that an idle king,
By this still hearth, among these barren crags,
Matched with an aged wife, I mete and dole
Unequal laws unto a savage race,
That hoard, and sleep, and feed, and know not me.
I cannot rest from travel: I will drink
Life to the lees: all times I have enjoy'd
Greatly, have suffer'd greatly, both with those
That loved me, and alone: on shore, and when
Thro' scudding drifts the rainy Hyades
Vext the dim sea: I am become a name;
For always roaming with a hungry heart
Much have I seen and known; cities of men
And manners, climates, councils, governments,
Myself not least, but honour'd of them all;
And drunk delight of battle with my peers,
Far on the ringing plains of windy Troy.

I am part of all that I have met;
Yet all experience is an arch wherethro'
Gleams that untravell'd world, whose margin fades
For ever and for ever when I move.
How dull it is to pause, to make an end,
To rust unburnish'd, not to shine in use!
As tho' to breathe were life. Life piled on life
Were all too little, and of one to me
Little remains; but every hour is saved
From that eternal silence, something more,
A bringer of new things; and vile it were
For some three suns to store and hoard myself,
And this gray spirit yearning in desire
To follow knowledge like a sinking star,
Beyond the utmost bound of human thought.

This is my son, mine own Telemachus,
To whom I leave the sceptre and the isle—
Well-loved of me, discerning to fulfil
This labour, by slow prudence to make mild
A rugged people, and thro' soft degrees
Subdue them to the useful and the good.
Most blameless is he, centred in the sphere
Of common duties, decent not to fail
In offices of tenderness, and pay
Meet adoration to my household gods
When I am gone. He works his work, I mine.
There lies the port; the vessel puffs her sail:
There gloom the dark broad seas. My mariners,
Souls that have toiled and wrought and thought with
    me—
That ever with a frolic welcome took
The thunder and the sunshine, and opposed
Free hearts, free foreheads—you and I are old;
Old age hath yet his honour and his toil;
Death closes all; but something ere the end,
Some work of noble note, may yet be done,
Not unbecoming men that strove with Gods.
The lights begin to twinkle from the rocks:
The long day wanes: the slow moon climbs: the deep
Moans round with many voices. Come, my friends,
'Tis not too late to seek a newer world.
Push off, and sitting well in order smite
The sounding furrows; for my purpose holds
To sail beyond the sunset, and the baths
Of all the western stars, until I die.

It may be that the gulfs will wash us down:
It may be we shall touch the Happy Isles,
And see the great Achilles, whom we knew.
Tho' much is taken, much abides; and tho'
We are not now that strength which in old days
Moved earth and heaven, that which we are, we are;
One equal temper of heroic hearts,
Made weak by time and fate, but strong in will
To strive, to seek, to find, and not to yield.

13

# CURIOSITY

ALASTAIR REID

may have killed the cat; more likely
the cat was just unlucky, or else curious
to see what death was like, having no cause
to go on licking paws, or fathering
litter on litter of kittens, predictably.

Nevertheless, to be curious
is dangerous enough. To distrust
what is always said, what seems,
to ask odd questions, interfere in dreams,
leave home, smell rats, have hunches,
cannot endear them to those doggy circles
where well-smelt baskets, suitable wives, good lunches
are the order of things, and where prevails
much wagging of incurious heads and tails.

Face it. Curiosity
will not cause him to die—
only lack of it will.
Never to want to see
the other side of the hill
or some improbable country
where living is an idyll
(although a probable hell)
would kill us all.
Only the curious
have, if they live, a tale
worth telling at all.

Dogs say cats love too much, are irresponsible,
are changeable, marry too many wives,
desert their children, chill all dinner tables
with tales of their nine lives.
Well, they are lucky. Let them be
nine-lived and contradictory,
curious enough to change, prepared to pay
the cat-price, which is to die
and die again and again,
each time with no less pain.

A cat minority of one
is all that can be counted on
to tell the truth. And what cats have to tell
on each return from hell
is this: that dying is what the living do,
that dying is what the loving do,
and that dead dogs are those who never know
that dying is what, to live, each has to do.

THE SWIMMER'S MOMENT

MARGARET AVISON

For everyone
The swimmer's moment at the whirlpool comes,
But many at that moment will not say
'This is the whirlpool, then.'
By their refusal they are saved
From the black pit, and also from contesting
The deadly rapids, and emerging in
The mysterious, and more ample, further waters.
And so their bland-blank faces turn and turn
Pale and forever on the rim of suction
They will not recognize.
Of those who dare the knowledge
Many are whirled into the ominous centre
That, gaping vertical, seals up
For them an eternal boon of privacy,
So that we turn away from their defeat
With a despair, not for their deaths, but for
Ourselves, who cannot penetrate their secret
Nor even guess at the anonymous breadth
Where one or two have won:
(The silver reaches of the estuary).

1960

NEW YEAR'S DAY, 1978

ELIZABETH BREWSTER

If I had thought forty years ago
when I asked myself where I would be
twenty—thirty—forty years from then—

If someone had told me then,
"On New Year's Day of 1978
you'll be sitting alone in a highrise apartment
in Saskatoon, Saskatchewan
writing a poem to yourself,"
how disappointed would I have been?

A fifteen-year-old romantic,
a brainy silly goose in love for the first time of many,
full of high ideals, religion, bad poetry, incurable shyness:
it's easy to laugh at myself as I was then
if I don't envy myself.

Fame, I thought.
Love, I thought.
Sons and daughters.
A big house with an orchard behind it.
Athens. Troy.
Heaven at the end, where I would meet my friends and
     relatives
miraculously young again.

I drink coffee, watch the smoke wreaths
rise above clustered branches,
imagine the delicate tracery
of hoarfrost on red berries.

I have lived all my life in rented rooms;
my loves have been temporary;
my best friends are dead;
I have no children.
I have yet to visit Troy (Where is it?)
My great book is still to be written.
I believe in God
only intermittently.
I live (like everyone else)
in fear of the destruction
of my country and my world.

Yet I would not change
these forty years,
would not omit depressions, wars, conflict,
death, pain,
or this solitude in which I drink coffee.

Smoke rises. The river flows under the ice.
There is a new blossom on my geranium.

A friend writes she is having a baby in July.
Next week I am giving a party.

Ten years from now
I may write my great book.
My lover may marry me
for my old-age pension.

In heaven I shall be a ballet dancer
creating perfect patterns
without words.

THE PERPETUAL MIGRATION

MARGE PIERCY

How do we know where we are going?
How do we know where we are headed
till we in fact or hope or hunch
arrive? You can only criticize,
the comfortable say, you don't know
what you want. Ah, but we do.

We have swung in the green verandas
of the jungle trees. We have squatted
on cloud-grey granite hillsides where
every leaf drips. We have crossed
badlands where the sun is sharp as flint.
We have paddled into the tall dark sea
in canoes. We always knew.

Peace, plenty, the gentle wallow
of intimacy, a bit of Saturday night
and not too much Monday morning,
a chance to choose, a chance to grow,
the power to say no and yes, pretties
and dignity, an occasional jolt of truth.

The human brain, wrinkled slug, knows
like a computer, like a violinist, like
a bloodhound, like a frog. We remember
backwards a little and sometimes forwards,
but mostly we think in the ebbing circles
a rock makes on the water.

The salmon hurtling upstream seeks
the taste of the waters of its birth
but the seabird on its four-thousand-mile
trek follows charts mapped on its genes.
The brightness, the angle, the sighting
of the stars shines in the brain luring
till inner constellation matches outer.

The stark black rocks, the island beaches
of waveworn pebbles where it will winter
look right to it. Months after it set
forth it says, home at last, and settles.
Even the pigeon beating its short whistling
wings knows the magnetic tug of arrival.

In my spine a tidal clock tilts and drips
and the moon pulls blood from my womb.
Driven as a migrating falcon, I can be blown
off course yet if I turn back it feels
wrong. Navigating by chart and chance
and passion I will know the shape
of the mountains of freedom, I will know.

THE DISCOVERY

GWENDOLYN MacEWEN

do not imagine that the exploration
ends, that she has yielded all her mystery
or that the map you hold
cancels further discovery

I tell you her uncovering takes years,
takes centuries, and when you find her naked
look again,
admit there is something else you cannot name,
a veil, a coating just above the flesh
which you cannot remove by your mere wish

when you see the land naked, look again
(burn your maps, that is not what I mean),
I mean the moment when it seems most plain
is the moment when you must begin again

1970

CHAPTER TWO

2 THE CHILD I WAS

THE POEMS

$\mathcal{P}$ALINDROME

LISEL MUELLER

"There is less difficulty—indeed, no logical difficulty at all—in imagining two portions of the universe, say two galaxies, in which time goes one way in one galaxy, and the opposite way in the other. . . . Intelligent beings in each galaxy would regard their own time as 'forward' and time in the other galaxy as 'backward.'"

MARTIN GARDNER, in Scientific American

Somewhere now she takes off the dress I am putting
on. It is evening in the anti-world, where she lives.
She is forty-five years away from her death, the hole
which spit her out into pain, impossible at first,
later easing, going, gone. She has unlearned much
by now. Her skin is firming, her memory sharpens,
her hair has grown glossy. She sees without glasses;
she falls in love easily. Her husband has lost his
shuffle; they laugh together. Their money shrinks,
but their ardor increases. Soon her second child
will be young enough to fight its way into her
body and change its life to monkey to frog to
tadpole to cluster of cells to tiny island
to nothing. She is making a list:

Things I will need in the past
   lipstick
   shampoo
   transistor radio
   Sergeant Pepper
   gel for blackheads
   5-year diary with lock

She is eager, having heard about
adolescent love and the freedom of
children. She wants to read *Crime and
Punishment* and ride on a roller-coaster
without getting sick. I think of her, as
she will be at fifteen, awkward, too serious.
In the mirror I see she uses her left hand to
write, her other to open a jar. By now our lives
should have crossed. Somewhere sometime we must
   have
passed one another like going and coming trains,
with both of us looking the other way.

*T*HE CHILD I WAS

MARIE-CLAIRE BLAIS
(*Trans. John Glassco*)

All that remains of childhood's fire
Is one burnt stone
And a thing that sometimes watches me
                    through nocturnal eyes,
A little ghost
In the pleading landscape,
A child over there, the child I was, maybe . . .

*B*ALLADE OF LOST OBJECTS

PHYLLIS McGINLEY

Where are the ribbons I tie my hair with?
   Where is my lipstick? Where are my hose—
The sheer ones hoarded these weeks to wear with
   Frocks the closets do not disclose?
Perfumes, petticoats, sports chapeaux,
   The blouse Parisian, the earring Spanish—
Everything suddenly ups and goes.
   And where in the world did the children vanish?

This is the house I used to share with
   Girls in pinafores, shier than does.
I can recall how they climbed my stair with
   Gales of giggles, on their tiptoes.
Last seen wearing both braids and bows
   (But looking rather Raggedy-Annish),
When they departed nobody knows—
   Where in the world did the children vanish?

Two tall strangers, now, I must bear with,
    Decked in my personal furbelows,
Raiding the larder, rending the air with
    Gossip and terrible radios.
Neither my friends nor quite my foes,
    Alien, beautiful, stern, and clannish,
Here they dwell, while the wonder grows:
    Where in the world did the children vanish?

Prince, I warn you, under the rose,
    Time is the thief you cannot banish.
These are my daughters, I suppose.
    But where in the world did the children vanish?

 *C*HILDHOOD

LORNA CROZIER

Close your eyes for a moment,
listen:
the floorboards groan at your mother's step,
bread pans scrape the oven grate,
her fingers tap the crust.
Where are you now?
Pretending sleep in another room
where windows turn dreams to frost,
feather forests, the birds are white
and make no sound.

Listen: your mother pours milk in a cup.
It holds the light like a small lamp,
draws shadows from her face.
Where have you gone?
Your mother is calling.
Your name is warmed by her breath.
Snow fills your tracks,
turns everything into a softer shape,
a silence, forgiveness.

Come in for supper,
it is growing dark.
A cup waits for you, a loaf of bread.
Your mother is calling, listen:
with her voice she builds a doorway
for you to enter, even now,
from such a long way off.

OTHERS

NIKKI GIOVANNI

the last time i was home
to see my mother we kissed
exchanged pleasantries
and unpleasantries pulled a warm
comforting silence around
us and read separate books

i remember the first time
i consciously saw her
we were living in a three room
apartment on burns avenue

mommy always sat in the dark
i don't know how i knew that but she did

that night i stumbled into the kitchen
maybe because i've always been
a night person or perhaps because i had wet
the bed
she was sitting on a chair
the room was bathed in moonlight diffused through
those thousands of panes landlords who rented
to people with children were prone to put in windows

she may have been smoking but maybe not
her hair was three-quarters her height
which made me a strong believer in the samson myth
and very black

i'm sure i just hung there by the door
i remember thinking: what a beautiful lady
she was very deliberately waiting
perhaps for my father to come home
from his night job or maybe for a dream
that had promised to come by
"come here" she said "i'll teach you
a poem: *i see the moon*
            the moon sees me
            god bless the moon
            and god bless me"
i taught it to my son
who recited it for her
just to say we must learn
to bear the pleasures
as we have borne the pains

THOSE WINTER SUNDAYS

ROBERT HAYDEN

Sundays too my father got up early
and put his clothes on in the blueblack cold,
then with cracked hands that ached
from labour in the weekday weather made
banked fires blaze. No one ever thanked him.

I'd wake and hear the cold splintering, breaking.
When the rooms were warm, he'd call,
and slowly I would rise and dress,
fearing the chronic angers of that house.

Speaking indifferently to him,
who had driven out the cold
and polished my good shoes as well.
What did I know, what did I know
of love's austere and lonely offices?

LETTER TO MY MOTHER

ANITA SKEEN

I remember when a Sunday friend and I,
bored with the good words of the morning and
the pleasantries of the noon meal,
escaped to the vacant lot behind our house
to play in the tall goldenrod
and hidden in the top branches of the persimmon tree,
antagonize small children
unable to catch hold of the lower limbs.

How we teased obnoxious Stevie Bull,
spit on him with sing-song poems
and ripe orange persimmons
till he ran screaming through the weeds,
a rodent harassed by the jays,
into the nest of his old stone house.

How, seconds later, his mother
erupted through the screen door, arms flailing,
eyes ripping leaves from the top of the trees,
her voice frenzied and crackling
with promises of retribution
more immediate and terrible
than those threats of eternal damnation
we had absorbed nonchalantly a few hours before.
I still feel her words crash
through the soft sunlight,
shatter the colors of the warm afternoon
and scatter the laughter like dry leaves in a storm.

How I dropped hard to the ground,
my heart banging against my ears, bursting
through the last tangled minutes onto the front porch,
each stride bringing nearer the ring
of the phone,
each breath adding
new lines to my story.

I do not remember what she said when she called,
what I said in defense or what
you said at all
and though there will be no more
angry mothers, no more Sunday games,
no more teasing of innocence
sometimes in still moments
that autumn terror
returns
leaves me stunned,
breathless,
naked in the garden
and I hear the steady ringing of the phone
into the long night.

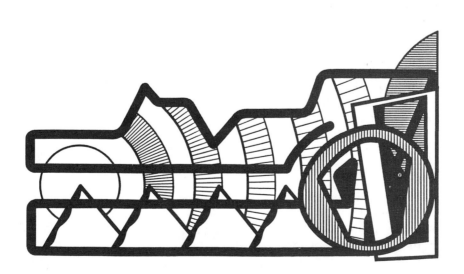

Coaster-Waggon on Indian Grove

RAYMOND SOUSTER

For my mother and father

Indian Grove was the name of the street then,
our house on the long block south of Humberside
starting out down a long hill, then smoothing out
after thirty yards or so. That already-sticky summer morning
with hot sidewalk under me, blazing sun above,
I sat with my legs crossed in my new coasting-waggon
at the top of the slope on the street's southeast corner,
both hands clutching the steering-handle very firmly,
with Joe Spring, my next-door conspirator
(looking forward to all the fun coming up in a minute),
starting in to push the waggon from behind,
slowly at first and then with all his might,

so that I ended up streaking down the hill
with a speed that made houses, front lawns, driveways,
blend in one flashing blur as my coaster-waggon rocked and
    swayed,
with me yelling out in terror when I couldn't steer it straight
    any more—
and, as if part of some larger heart-rending plan,
with my waggon now a crazed thing out of all control,
it shot off the pavement not far from where the slope levelled
    out,
first pitching me, then tumbling me like some awkward
    whirling ball
down under the unsuspecting feet of an old horse hitched
to an Ideal bread-waggon stopped unfortunately for me
at that very same spot. And naturally that animal
couldn't help but panic, reared up with a startled whinny,
more in self-defence than in anger at this strange object
    thrown
at its feet without warning or good reason—
so that unluckily for me (though it could have been worse),
one sharp front hoof ended up stamping lightly down
on the right side of my forehead—

and when I finally opened my eyes again
(it seemed hours later),
with the whole world doing a wobbly whirling round and
    round
like a top that couldn't stop spinning,
I was in my father's arms, with him yelling wildly
like I'd never heard before at the poor bread-waggon driver.
But when he saw my now-opened, tear-freshened eyes,
he smiled down at me as he very seldom smiled,
and I knew it was all right, that I wouldn't be punished,
and that I'd never coast down that hill again
as long as I lived on that West End Toronto street . . . .

And I never did, or even wanted to.

*B*APTISM

DALE ZIEROTH

In mid-river we join the ancient force
of mud and leaves moving in their journey
down the face of the continent and after
the first dance of leaving
one element for another, we fall quiet,
waiting for the silence to give us a
glimpse of history. In mid-river, it is
still possible to imagine Thompson's world,
without roads or bridges, rivers that
go back beyond white lives into the rocks
that push and fold, fault and break
as the new world rises from
the old.
       Yet this is still our river.
It does not matter that we are not
the first, what we will find today
has been found a hundred times before: it is
the ancient story of men meeting water,
as if there were a time, or faith,
when all of us were rivers, one
strength sliding out of the sky and into
the sea, one direction in us all.

But the river churns here and beats along the shore.
It picks up speed on the outside curve
cutting past the cottonwoods and under the deadfalls
that sweep across the water like the last arm of the land
and the water takes command.
I bend my paddle in my hand and my friend
digs in but there are branches like dead fingers in our faces
and there can be
no avoidance now, water comes up up and the
snag bends us down until my lungs
are in the water they are stones and I am

grabbing for the tree as if it were
my friend while the current sucks on me and my arms
go heavy as lead, a scream
goes dead in my throat, we do not
belong here, it bubbles and swallows
silt, the taste of ice,
there are blue stars somewhere and all the sounds of water
are alive and they pour in my ears,
into my eyes as if the river is already sure
how deep it will carry me,
what it will do with my skin, how it will dissolve
and burst and thin out the blood and I roll over
in a dream of clouds, willows, catch the edge
of a bank beaver's hole, brown mud like gold on my palm,
my feet still pulling for the ocean and then they find
gravel, the river rock, the river
pushes me away and I am shaking in the air again,
shaking for my friend riding the canoe's bottom
like a drunken pea pod, he grinds on the bank
a hundred yards downstream, his boots sucked off,
his body like a hole in the sand.

I breathe in the sun, take it yellow
into the body that spits grey in the river.
The baptism is over.
We have walked away without the grace of
fish or grebes, and the river is still the same.
I sit and watch the water with the oldest eyes of men:
if I trust the river, I will be
caught in it, rolled backwards into the
simplest race of all, the first, and the river is hard, it is
carnal and twists like an animal going blind in the rain,
but it leaves me pouring water from my shoe and then I see
him stand, wave, we have
first words.
Soon our paddles will bite the water but they will not
break it: our place on earth is rich enough,
the sudden rush of birdsong, our own
mid-river laughter as the warmth begins again.

 # LETTING GO

DAWN STAR FIRE

Funny how you never
   really give up on your dreams,
      and yet they seem to move farther away,
         with every passing year.

It's kind of like
   burning your nose on the toaster,
      because you have cigarettes, but no matches,
   and yet, when you finally remember
      to buy the matches,
         you can't afford the cigarettes.

It's all a matter of timing,
   like waiting twenty-two months
      for you to come home,
        and then leaving
           when you arrive . . .

$\mathcal{T}$HE PROPOSAL

EVA TIHANYI

or A Variation on "The Anniversary" by Magritte

It happened when she was young,
when there were things she wanted to know,
edges she wanted to walk along with words,
longings she curved into

She planned to leave home, he wanted to marry her:
two ideas amiably complected—or so it seemed

Then she started seeing things:

> the books piled, unread, on her dresser;
> the dances hidden in her bedside radio;
> the green outside withering into brown;
> everything losing lustre

He did not notice
that her face turned slowly into stone, grew
until it filled the frame of his vision

She wrote letters to herself, spent hours
thinking of words with which to think;
then she began to say
and the saying changed her

She told him she wanted
the world windowing open around her,
the wild lemon sun squeezing itself in

She told him dreams of white stucco villas
on the tips of Greek islands,
high-ceilinged brownstones on old Parisian streets

He spoke of rings and calendars
as her face turned suddenly light,
lifted skyward, away from him

I DREAMED A DREAM

HERBERT KRETZMER

(Original in French by Alain Boublil and Jean-Marc Natel)

There was a time when men were kind
When their voices were soft
And their words inviting.
There was a time when love was blind
And the world was a song
And the song was exciting.
There was a time.
Then it all went wrong.

I dreamed a dream in time gone by
When hope was high
And life worth living
I dreamed that love would never die
I dreamed that God would be forgiving.

Then I was young and unafraid
And dreams were made, and used,
And wasted
There was no ransom to be paid
No song unsung
No wine untasted.

But the tigers come at night
With their voices soft as thunder
As they tear your hope apart
As they turn your dream to shame

He slept a summer by my side
He filled my days
With endless wonder
He took my childhood in his stride
But he was gone when autumn came.

And still I dream he'll come to me
That we will live the years together
But there are dreams that cannot be
And there are storms we cannot weather.

I had a dream my life would be
So different from this hell I'm living
So different now from what it seemed
Now life has killed
The dream I dreamed.

READING THE BROTHERS GRIMM TO JENNY

LISEL MUELLER

Jenny, your mind commands
kingdoms of black and white:
you shoulder the crow on your left,
the snowbird on your right;
for you the cinders part
and let the lentils through,
and noise falls into place
as screech or sweet roo-coo,
while in my own, real, world
gray foxes and gray wolves
bargain eye to eye,
and the amazing dove
takes shelter under the wing
of the raven to keep dry.

Knowing that you must climb,
one day, the ancient tower
where disenchantment binds
the curls of innocence,
that you must live with power
and honor circumstance,
that choice is what comes true—
oh, Jenny, pure in heart,
why do I lie to you?

Why do I read you tales
in which birds speak the truth
and pity cures the blind,
and beauty reaches deep
to prove a royal mind?
Death is a small mistake
there, where the kiss revives;
Jenny, we make just dreams
out of our unjust lives.

Still, when your truthful eyes,
your keen, attentive stare,
endow the vacuous slut
with royalty, when you match
her soul to her shimmering hair,
what can she do but rise
to your imagined throne?
And what can I, but see
beyond the world that is,
when, faithful, you insist
I have the golden key—
and learn from you once more
the terror and the bliss,
the world as it might be?

GAME CALLED ON ACCOUNT OF DARKNESS

PETER VIERECK

Once there was a friend.
He watched me from the sky.
Maybe he never lived at all.
Maybe too much friendship made him die.

When the gang played cops-and-robbers in the alley,
It was my friend who told me which were which,
Now he doesn't tell me any more.
(Which team am I playing for?)

My science teacher built a telescope
To show me every answer in the end.
I stared and stared at every star for hours.
I couldn't find my friend.

At Sunday School they said I breathe too much.
When I hold my breath within the under
Side of earth, they said I'll find my friend.
. . . I wonder.

He was like a kind of central heating
In the big cold house, and that was good.
One by one I have to chop my toys now,
As firewood.

Everytime I stood upon a crossroads,
It made me mad to feel him watch me choose.
I'm glad there's no more spying while I play.
Still, I'm sad he went away.

NORTH STAR

ZONA GALE

His boy had stolen some money from a booth
At the County Fair. I found the father in his kitchen.
For years he had driven a dray and the heavy lifting
Had worn him down. So through his evenings
He slept by the kitchen stove as I found him.
The mother was crying and ironing.
I thought about the mother,
For she brought me a photograph
Taken at a street fair on her wedding day.
She was so trim and white and he so neat and alert.
In the picture with their friends about them—
I saw that she wanted me to know their dignity from the
first.
But afterward I thought more about the father.
For as he came with me to the door
I could not forbear to say how bright and near the
stars seemed.
Then he leaned and peered from beneath his low roof
And he said:
"There used to be a star called the Nord Star."

GRADUATION EVENING

ELIZABETH BREWSTER

I remember the night of high-school graduation:
the nervous, sixth-time combing of hair before a mirror
in the classroom turned dressing-room; girls refastening
belts and collars, telling each other how skirts hung.
Someone restlessly played with chalk, and dropped a boxfull.
In the hallway leading to the auditorium
the music teacher beat ta-tum tum-ta:
Can't you keep time, for once, to the beat of the music?
The pointer tapped on the floor, the head nodded.

Then we marched through the rows of waiting parents,
heads up, military in this year of war.
We sat on the platform, rigid, remembering not to cross our
knees.
They played *God Save the King* and *Rule Britannia*.
Somebody made a speech about the war,
and all life being a war, and carrying torches.
Prizes were handed out, diplomas rustled.
They made us sing—what was it? *Alouette*?

I remember that night, going to bed, tired,
wetting my pillow with a flood of tears.
For what? I can't remember. Maybe not winning
a prize I wanted, maybe winning one
I didn't care for.
                    Maybe suddenly,
I was frightened, knowing that the classroom
with chalk, globes, books, and blackboard, maps and desks
was floating out to sea, ungraspable;
and I was left, as the man had said,
with life as a war
and the world
                    an exploding time bomb
                                        in my hands.

AGE OLD WISDOM

LOUIS GINSBERG

Though newscasters warn us
    We must take heed in
Times that ripen
    Not as in Eden;

Though diplomats' pouches
    Are bulging with headlines,
And jet-planes hurry
    Crises to deadlines,

Lovers and babies
    Come unfraid,
Into a world
    They never made.

Life is ever,
    Since man was born,
Licking honey
    From a thorn.

EXPERIENCE

DOROTHY LIVESAY

"For your own good" they said,
And they gave me bread
Bitter and hard to swallow.
My head felt tired after it,
My heart felt hollow.

So I went away on my own road
Tasting all fruits, all breads:
And if some were bitter, others were sweet—
So I learned
How the heart is fed.

$\mathcal{W}$ITH AGE, WISDOM

ARCHIBALD MacLEISH

At twenty, stooping round about,
I thought the world a miserable place,
Truth a trick, faith in doubt,
Little beauty, less grace.

Now at sixty what I see,
Although the world is worse by far,
Stops my heart in ecstasy.
God, the wonders that there are!

$\mathcal{B}$EAUTIFUL OLD AGE

D.H. LAWRENCE

It ought to be lovely to be old
to be full of the peace that comes of experience
and wrinkled ripe fulfilment.

The wrinkled smile of completeness that follows a life
lived undaunted and unsoured with accepted lies.
If people lived without accepting lies
they would ripen like apples, and be scented like
pippins
in their old age.

Soothing, old people should be, like apples
when one is tired of love.
Fragrant like yellowing leaves, and dim with the soft
stillness and satisfaction of autumn.

And a girl should say:
It must be wonderful to live and grow old.
Look at my mother, how rich and still she is!—

And a young man should think: By Jove
my father has faced all weathers, but it's been a
    life!—

3 *A* STRANGER NOW

THE POEMS

ON LONELINESS

ANNE SZUMIGALSKI

The question is always the same:
Did you decide to leave me,
Or did I decide to remain here alone?

And what is alone? A white sky,
An empty hill, a forest without leaves?

A house with one chair, one cup
One bent knife, a narrow bed,
One coat on one peg.

From the first day I knew I must begin
To talk to myself, for fear of forgetting

The sound, the use of words.
For fear that for me they would become

Mere bird-scratches on paper,
Botanist's Latin on a page of notes.

When a word describes, tell me does it become
The thing described? Is distance itself

The sound of the word—*distance, distance*?

Wherever you are, why don't you
Turn and look back across that distance,

And see the ocean stretching, and the land,
Mountainous, and flat.

And see the forest
Where we were together.

Tell me, what is a forest
But so many single trees

Each clattering its bony branches in the wind,
Each standing among its fallen companions.

NONE OF THE OTHER BIRDS

STEVIE SMITH

None of the other birds seem to like it
It sits alone on the corner edge of the outhouse gutter
They do not even dislike it
Enough to bite it
So it sits alone unbitten
It is always alone.

SANCTUARY

DOROTHY PARKER

My land is bare of chattering folk;
   The clouds are low along the ridges,
And sweet's the air with curly smoke
   From all my burning bridges.

# ALONE

JONATHAN HOLDEN

Alone is delicious.
There's no one to see.
I can eat these low clouds
and the body of wind
that's turning them into rolling
tumbleweed, eat with my hands,
get crumbs over everything,
crumbs of clouds on my nose,
in my fingernails, clouds smeared
all over my shirt and my chin,
I can lick the clouds off my fingers
and no one can see or care if
I have as much dessert as I want.
I just reach into those blue
holes that I've left and pull out
whole fistfuls of sky, of infinity.
It's tasteless and so hard
I can chew it for hours.

# LONELINESS

EMMA LaROCQUE

Ah loneliness,
How would I know
Who I am
Without you?

SOLITUDE

ARCHIBALD LAMPMAN

How still it is here in the woods. The trees
   Stand motionless, as if they do not dare
   To stir, lest it should break the spell. The air
Hangs quiet as spaces in a marble frieze.
Even this little brook, that runs at ease,
   Whispering and gurgling in its knotted bed,
   Seems but to deepen with its curling thread
Of sound the shadowy sun-pierced silences.

Sometimes a hawk screams or a woodpecker
   Startles the stillness from its fixèd mood
With his loud careless tap. Sometimes I hear
    The dreamy white-throat from some far-off tree
Pipe slowly on the listening solitude
    His five pure notes succeeding pensively.

SPRING QUIET

CHRISTINA ROSSETTI

Gone were but the Winter,
   Come were but the Spring
I would go to a covert
   Where the birds sing.

Where in the whitethorn
   Singeth a thrush,
And a robin sings
   In the holly bush.

Full of fresh scents
   Are the budding boughs
Arching high over
   A cool green house:

Full of sweet scents,
   And whispering air
Which sayeth softly:
   'We spread no snare;

'Here dwell in safety,
   Here dwell alone,
With a clear stream
   And a mossy stone.

'Here the sun shineth
   Most shadily;
Here is heard an echo
   Of the far sea,
Though far off it be.'

THE WILD SWANS AT COOLE

WILLIAM BUTLER YEATS

The trees are in their autumn beauty,
The woodland paths are dry,
Under the October twilight the water
Mirrors a still sky;
Upon the brimming water among the stones
Are nine-and-fifty swans

The nineteenth autumn has come upon me
Since I first made my count;
I saw, before I had well finished,
All suddenly mount
And scatter wheeling in great broken rings
Upon their clamorous wings.

I have looked upon those brilliant creatures,
And now my heart is sore.
All's changed since I, hearing at twilight,
The first time on this shore,
The bell-beat of their wings above my head,
Trod with a lighter tread.

Unwearied still, lover by lover,
They paddle in the cold
Companionable streams or climb the air;
Their hearts have not grown old;
Passion or conquest, wander where they will,
Attend upon them still.

But now they drift on the still water
Mysterious, beautiful;
Among what rushes will they build,
By what lake's edge or pool
Delight men's eyes when I awake some day
To find they have flown away?

# RYOKAN

ANDREW WREGGITT

Sometimes it is this simple
A Japanese girl in the bath,
the sound of water
moving in her hands,
her thin, high voice, singing
Each note carried up, mournful, longing
The intimacy of breath and steam

Sometimes, it is this simple
A single listener carried up
in these motionless rooms
by the slow notes of a young girl's song,
by the loneliness we share
The child who is in us
and never leaves

Sometimes, the delicate bones
of a girl's hands, wandering aimlessly
A single wavering note released
through the thin walls of this inn
Delicate leaves in the garden
turn and turn in the light,
the stilled afternoon

Sometimes there is a single note
of our own youth
wavering in a closed room
The first cicadas of evening
beginning,
calling down the distant memory
of the stars

$\mathcal{P}$IANO MAN

BILLY JOEL

It's nine o'clock on a Saturday,
The regular crowd shuffles in.
There's an old man sitting next to me
Making love to his tonic and gin.

He says, son, can you play me a memory,
I'm not really sure how it goes,
But it's sad and it's sweet
And I knew it complete
When I wore a younger man's clothes.

Sing us a song, you're the piano man,
Sing us a song tonight.
Well, we're all in the mood for a melody,
And you've got us feeling all right.

Now, John at the bar is a friend of mine,
He gives me my drinks for free,
And he's quick with a joke
Or to light up a smoke,
But there's some place that he'd rather be.

He says, Bill, I believe this is killing me,
As a smile ran away from his face,
But I'm sure that I could be a movie star
If I could get out of this place.

Now, Paul is a real estate novelist
Who never had time for a wife,
And he's talking with David
Who's still in the navy
And probably will be for life.

And the waitress is practicing politics
As the businessmen slowly get stoned.
Yes, they're sharing a drink they call loneliness,
But it's better than drinking alone.

Sing us a song, you're the piano man,
Sing us a song tonight.
Well, we're all in the mood for a melody,
And you've got us feeling all right.

It's a pretty good crowd for a Saturday,
And the manager gives me a smile
Cause he knows that it's me
That they've been coming to see
To forget about life for a while.

And the piano sounds like a carnival,
And the microphone smells like beer,
And they sit at the bar
And put bread in my jar
And say, man, what are you doing here?

Sing us a song, you're the piano man,
Sing us a song tonight.
Well, we're all in the mood for a melody,
And you've got us feeling all right.

DANGLING CONVERSATION

PAUL SIMON

It's a still life water color
of a now late afternoon
as the sun shines through the curtain lace
and shadows wash the room
and we sit and drink our coffee
casting our indifference
like shells upon the shore
you can hear the ocean roar
in the dangling conversation
and the superficial sighs
the borders of our lives.

And you read your Emily Dickinson
and I my Robert Frost
and we note our place with bookmarkers
that measure what we've lost
like a poem poorly written
we are verses out of rhythm
couplets out of rhyme
in syncopated time
and the dangling conversation
and the superficial sighs
are the borders of our lives.

Yes, we speak of things that matter
with words that must be said
can analysis be worthwhile
is the theatre really dead
and how the room is softly faded
and I only kiss your shadow
I cannot feel your hand
you're a stranger now unto me
lost in the dangling conversation
and the superficial sighs
in the borders of our lives.

THE LOVE SONG OF
J. ALFRED PRUFROCK

T.S. ELIOT

S'io credesse che mia risposta fosse
A persona che mai tornasse al mondo,
Questa fiamma staria senza piu scosse.
Ma perciocche giammai di questo fondo
Non torno vivo alcun, s'i'odo il vero,
Senza tema d'infamia ti rispondo.

Let us go then, you and I,
When the evening is spread out against the sky
Like a patient etherized upon a table;
Let us go, through certain half-deserted streets,
The muttering retreats
Of restless nights in one-night cheap hotels
And sawdust restaurants with oyster-shells:
Streets that follow like a tedious argument
Of insidious intent
To lead you to an overwhelming question . . . .
Oh, do not ask, "What is it?"
Let us go and make our visit.

In the room the women come and go
Talking of Michelangelo.

The yellow fog that rubs its back upon the window-panes,
The yellow smoke that rubs its muzzle on the window-panes
Licked its tongue into the corners of the evening,
Lingered upon the pools that stand in drains,
Let fall upon its back the soot that falls from chimneys,
Slipped by the terrace, made a sudden leap,
And seeing that it was a soft October night,
Curled once about the house, and fell asleep.

And indeed there will be time
For the yellow smoke that slides along the street
Rubbing its back upon the window-panes;
There will be time, there will be time
To prepare a face to meet the faces that you meet;
There will be time to murder and create,

And time for all the works and days of hands
That lift and drop a question on your plate;
Time for you and time for me,
And time yet for a hundred indecisions,
And for a hundred visions and revisions,
Before the taking of a toast and tea.

In the room the women come and go
Talking of Michelangelo.

And indeed there will be time
To wonder, "Do I dare?" and, "Do I dare?"
Time to turn back and descend the stair,
With a bald spot in the middle of my hair—
(They will say: "How his hair is growing thin!")
My morning coat, my collar mounting firmly to the chin,
My necktie rich and modest, but asserted by a simple pin—
(They will say: "But how his arms and legs are thin!")
Do I dare
Disturb the universe?
In a minute there is time
For decisions and revisions which a minute will reverse.

For I have known them all already, known them all:
Have known the evenings, mornings, afternoons,
I have measured out my life with coffee spoons;
I know the voices dying with a dying fall
Beneath the music from a farther room.
   So how should I presume?

And I have known the eyes already, known them all—
The eyes that fix you in a formulated phrase,
And when I am formulated, sprawling on a pin,
When I am pinned and wriggling on the wall,
Then how should I begin
To spit out all the butt-ends of my days and ways?
   And how should I presume?

And I have known the arms already, known them all—
Arms that are braceleted and white and bare
(But in the lamplight, downed with light brown hair!)
Is it perfume from a dress
That makes me so digress?
Arms that lie along a table, or wrap about a shawl.
   And should I then presume?
   And how should I begin?

Shall I say, I have gone at dusk through narrow streets
And watched the smoke that rises from the pipes
Of lonely men in shirt-sleeves, leaning out of windows? . . .

I should have been a pair of ragged claws
Scuttling across the floors of silent seas.

And the afternoon, the evening, sleeps so peacefully!
Smoothed by long fingers,
Asleep . . . tired . . . or it malingers,
Stretched on the floor, here beside you and me.
Should I, after tea and cakes and ices,
Have the strength to force the moment to its crisis?
But though I have wept and fasted, wept and prayed,
Though I have seen my head (grown slightly bald) brought in upon a
    platter,
I am no prophet—and here's no great matter;
I have seen the moment of my greatness flicker,
And I have seen the eternal Footman hold my coat, and snicker,
And in short, I was afraid.

And would it have been worth it, after all,
After the cups, the marmalade, the tea.
Among the porcelain, among some talk of you and me,
Would it have been worth while,
To have bitten off the matter with a smile,
To have squeezed the universe into a ball
To roll it toward some overwhelming question,
To say: "I am Lazarus, come from the dead,
Come back to tell you all, I shall tell you all"—
If one, settling a pillow by her head,
    Should say: "That is not what I meant at all;
    That is not it, at all."

And would it have been worth it, after all,
Would it have been worth while,
After the sunsets and the dooryards and the sprinkled streets,
After the novels, after the teacups, after the skirts that trail along the
    floor—
And this, and so much more?—

It is impossible to say just what I mean!
But as if a magic lantern threw the nerves in patterns on a screen:
Would it have been worth while
If one, settling a pillow or throwing off a shawl,
And turning toward the window, should say:
    "That is not it at all,
    That is not what I meant, at all."

No! I am not Prince Hamlet, nor was meant to be;
Am an attendant lord, one that will do
To swell a progress, start a scene or two,
Advise the prince; no doubt, an easy tool,
Deferential, glad to be of use,
Politic, cautious, and meticulous;
Full of high sentence, but a bit obtuse;
At times, indeed, almost ridiculous—
Almost, at times, the Fool.

I grow old. . . . I grow old. . . .
I shall wear the bottoms of my trousers rolled.

Shall I part my hair behind? Do I dare to eat a peach?
I shall wear white flannel trousers, and walk upon the beach.
I have heard the mermaids singing, each to each.

I do not think that they will sing to me.

I have seen them riding seaward on the waves
Combing the white hair of the waves blown back
When the wind blows the water white and black.

We have lingered in the chambers of the sea
By sea-girls wreathed with seaweed red and brown
Till human voices wake us, and we drown.

NOT WAVING BUT DROWNING

STEVIE SMITH

Nobody heard him, the dead man,
But still he lay moaning:
I was much further out than you thought
And not waving but drowning.

Poor chap, he always loved larking
And now he's dead
It must have been too cold for him his heart gave way,
They said.

Oh, no no no, it was too cold always
(Still the dead one lay moaning)
I was much too far out all my life
And not waving but drowning.

A NOTE ON THE PUBLIC TRANSPORTATION SYSTEM

ALDEN NOWLAN

It's not hard to begin
a conversation with the person
who happens to be seated
nearest you, especially when she's been
reading with apparent interest
a book that's one of your
favourites and can't find
her matches.
                    The difficulty is
once you've spoken you can never
go back to being comfortable
with silence,
                    even if you learn
you've nothing to say
and would rather not listen.
                    You can stop talking
but you can't forget
the broken wires
dangling there between you.
                    You'll smile almost guiltily
when your glances
accidentally bump.
                    It may get so bad
that one of you will have to
pretend to fall asleep.

40 ——— LOVE

ROGER McGOUGH

middle	aged
couple	playing
ten	nis
when	the
game	ends
and	they
go	home
the	net
will	still
be	be
tween	them

ALLS

CONSTANTINE P. CAVAFY
(*Trans. Rae Dalven*)

Without consideration, without pity, without shame
they have built big and high walls around me.

And now I sit here despairing.
I think of nothing else: this fate gnaws at my mind;

for I had many things to do outside.
Ah why didn't I observe them when they were building the walls?

But I never heard the noise or the sound of the builders.
Imperceptibly they shut me out of the world.

EGARDING A DOOR

DAVID ANTIN

regarding a door
its open and shut
but it is less open and shut than a wall
a wall is something to lean on
and its unwise to lean on a door
regarding a door
you can take it in hand
turning the knob of a door you can open it and step through
then its no longer a door
now in the case of a wall
its a wall wherever you are
which is evident and consoling
with a wall you always know where you are
while a door is only a door from outside
there is also something substantial about walls
maybe its the materials from which theyre made
the bricks and the plaster
but more likely its the absence of hinges
the hinges in doors are like hidden conditions
upon which everything turns
theyre like the small print in contracts
a door depends on its hinges

WHERE THERE'S A WALL

JOY KOGAWA

Where there's a wall
there's a way through a
gate or door. There's even
a ladder perhaps and a
sentinel who sometimes sleeps.
There are secret passwords you
can overhear. There are methods
of torture for extracting clues
to maps of underground passages.
There are zeppelins, helicopters,
rockets, bombs, battering rams,
armies with trumpets whose
all at once blast shatters
the foundations.

Where there's a wall there are
words to whisper by loose bricks,
wailing prayers to utter, birds
to carry messages taped to their feet.
There are letters to be written—
poems even.

Faint as in a dream
is the voice that calls
from the belly
of the wall.

4 THE HUMAN TOUCH

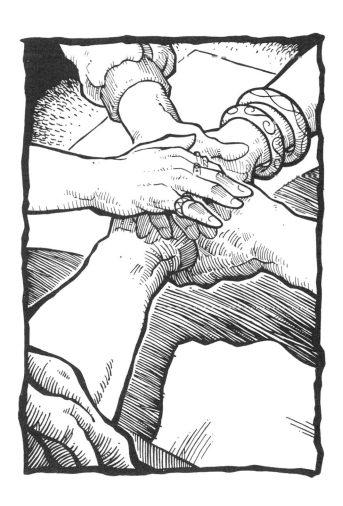

THE POEMS

AT A WINDOW

CARL SANDBURG

Give me hunger,
O you gods that sit and give
The world its orders.
Give me hunger, pain and want;
Shut me out with shame and failure
From your doors of gold and fame,
Give me your shabbiest, weariest hunger.

But leave me a little love,
A voice to speak to me in the day end,
A hand to touch me in the dark room
Breaking the long loneliness.
In the dusk of day-shapes
Blurring the sunset,
One little wandering, western star
Thrust out from the changing shores of shadow.
Let me go to the window,
Watch there the day-shapes of dusk,
And wait and know the coming
Of a little love.

65

THE HUMAN TOUCH

SPENCER MICHAEL FREE

'Tis the human touch in this world that counts,
   The touch of your hand and mine,
Which means far more to the fainting heart
   Than shelter and bread and wine;
For shelter is gone when the night is o'er,
   And bread lasts only a day,
But the touch of the hand and the sound of the voice
   Sing on in the soul alway.

BEDTIME

DENISE LEVERTOV

We are a meadow where the bees hum,
mind and body are almost one

as the fire snaps in the stove
and our eyes close,

and mouth to mouth, the covers
pulled over our shoulders,

we drowse as horses drowse afield,
in accord; though the fall cold

surrounds our warm bed, and though
by day we are singular and often lonely.

NO MAN IS AN ISLAND

JOHN DONNE

No man is an island, entire of itself:
Every man is a piece of the continent,
A part of the main.
If a clod be washed away by the sea,
Europe is the less,
As well as if a promontory were,
As well as if a manor of thy friend
Or of thine own, were.
Any man's death diminishes me,
Because I am involved in mankind;
And, therefore, never send to know
For whom the bell tolls:
It tolls for thee.

THE HAND

BRIAN FAWCETT

Trees,
and the wind,
the moon rising out of the southwest
over the calm lagoon

like a Joseph Conrad story,
nightbirds and all that,
the traditional things of poetry
at hand.

But the pleasure of it
trickles through my hands,
the old sense of beauty
feels perverse, and slipping through
the mossy pickets of the old delight
a stench now carries on the wind.

Conrad's tropic palms here
are common firs in shadow, both
are rooted in a dark
that whispers, like beauty does,
because the things we live with every day and take for
    granted
are rooted in the degradation of this planet
and the misery of countless human beings.

In the mostly private tangle poetry has fallen to,
I want to force the appearance of these shadows
to slime the Beautiful with facts
like those of the systematic murder in the Congo
of as many as twenty-five million people
between 1890 and 1910:

facts not secondary to
nor separate from
the leisure to write poems
or even watch the moonrise on a summer's evening.

I'm thinking of the battered amber wings
of a butterfly my son rescued from a tangle of weeds
just this afternoon, proudly cupped to show me
in his two small hands.

For him if nothing else
I want to evoke these factual disturbances
in the act of thinking and writing
until what I've learned as beauty
becomes accountable to
the terrifying facts of the world

or if those facts are to be partitioned
from the concerns of Art
then Art must be recognized
and condemned
as an accomplice
in maintaining the conditions
that make misery and violence
the dominant experience of most human lives.

I want to learn
to turn my hand against mere beauty
until such facts are a bad memory
unthinkable in the acts of living men and women.

I told my son to let the butterfly go
that it has a message to deliver
in the several days of life it has

that nothing beautiful
should be made a captive.

He smiled, then opened up his hands to let it go:
it spilled out, fell into the weeds once more
but then it flitted, it took flight. See?

I've let the butterfly exist
no longer an event of isolated poesy
removed from the twenty-five million Africans
murdered in the economic service of what was set up
   by the European powers and the U.S.
as a "free state"
under the sadistic governance of Leopold II of Belgium
who used the proceeds of the rubber trade
to buy the finest art of Europe
repatriating the Flemish Masters
and filling the museums
any number of us
have wandered through in awe.

As the shadows descend across the lagoon
the news on television shows us
footage of another war in Africa,

And there are whistles in the dark, too many things
so easy to believe or conjure up
or fall before in worship or in fear.

What matter that butterflies drift
across the path of the descending moon?
What songs do the nightbirds sing for us?
Do we hear what they really have to tell us?

Who captains this craft
across the nightmare beauty hides?

What should I do
with these hands?

from *A* CONTINUAL INTEREST IN THE SUN AND SEA

KEITH GUNDERSON

A GAME CALLED
TRYING TO DISCERN
THE INDIVIDUAL JOURNEY: or try to keep your eye on
                              a single wave coming in
                              pick any wave coming in

                                 go on,
                                 go on,
                                 pick one:

                                 now

                                 try to keep
                              your eye on
                                 your eye on
                                    your
                                       eye
                                             on
                                       on

                                    it

                           is   it

                                    still
                              the very wave
                                    you'd
                                       picked?

        (for those who do not
          live near the sea
            use a leaf
              or a flake
                of snow
                  fall-
                    ing

GRACIOUS GOODNESS

MARGE PIERCY

On the beach where we had been idly
telling the shell coins
cat's paw, cross-barred Venus, china cockle,
we both saw at once
the sea bird fall to the sand
and flap grotesquely.
He had taken a great barbed hook
out through the cheek and fixed
in the big wing.
He was pinned to himself to die,
a royal tern with a black crest blown back
as if he flew in his own private wind.
He felt good in my hands, not fragile
but muscular and glossy and strong,
the beak that could have split my hand
opening only to cry
as we yanked on the barbs.
We borrowed a clippers, cut and drew out the hook.
Then the royal tern took off, wavering,
lurched twice,
then acrobat returned to his element, dipped,
zoomed, and sailed out to dive for a fish.
Virtue: what a sunrise in the belly.
Why is there nothing
I have ever done with anybody
that seems to me so obviously right?

*P*OEM

AL PURDY

You are ill and so I lead you away
and put you to bed in the dark room
—you lie breathing softly and I hold your hand
feeling the fingertips relax as sleep comes

You will not sleep more than a few hours
and the illness is less serious than any anger or cruelty
and the dark bedroom is like a foretaste of other darknesses
to come later which all of us must endure alone
but here I am permitted to be with you

After a while in sleep your fingers clutch tightly
and I know that whatever may be happening
the fear coiled in dreams or the bright trespass of pain
there is nothing at all I can do except hold your hand
and not go away

1971

*W*INTER FIREFLIES

STEPHEN BROCKWELL

Static sparks raise my hair as I take off my shirt
in my dry, electrically heated room.
The window creaks in a tide of wind and snow;
weather warnings are broadcast on the radio.
Only streetlights and trees are wavered by the wind.

Fishtailing around the corner, a car
skids off a patch of ice into the ditch.
The car door opens like a palpitating gill.
The driver emerges.

                Under the streetlight,
in a current of driving snow, flakes collect
on his hair and shoulders like particles of steel.
The flakes ignite as he lights a cigarette.

I will dress, go out, and help him move his car,
pushing through the white swarm of winter fireflies.

OLD FRIENDS MEET

GLEN SORESTAD

for Alden Nowlan

We meet again after several years
and clasp each other like reunited lovers.

Perhaps two aging professional wrestlers
would be more precise, except that here

there is no competition at all. Only
a coming together of kindred spirits

bound each to the other by some
bond so mysterious and magical

there is no need for words.
Perhaps in this electric silence,

lies contentment, sealed by the warmth
of fraternal touch, the physical bond.

Neither distance nor the grave can
dim that wondrous and unspoken knowing

that we shared. Fellow wrestler,
poet and brother.

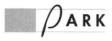ARK

DAVID IGNATOW

I sit beside old retired Italians.
They chat and have smooth skins.
Their hair is white, and the flesh full.
They make no disturbance.
They rest all day, sitting in a park.
One will come over from his house
and add to the crowd.
                    They never
grow loud. They talk and laugh,
solid company every day. I love
to come here and sit with them,
I a stranger, and feel the quiet
and stability they make,
and lasting custom.

IRST LOVE

JUDITH HEMSCHEMEYER

We fell in love at "Journey for Margaret,"
my mother and I. I was the same age
as Margaret O'Brien, braids and all

and she put her arm on the back of my chair
and touched my head and found the lump
I'd got that morning and forgot I had.

"What's this?" she whispered and I whispered back
I'd cracked my head against the brick wall
of the Savings and Loan walking backwards to school.

And the waves of her giggles washed over me
there in the dark. I had astonished her!
No telling what I'd do next!

But whatever it was, I knew that from then on
what happened between us was just as important
as Margaret O'Brien getting adopted up there on the screen.

SIGNATURE

HANNAH KAHN

If I sing because I must
being made of singing dust,

and I cry because of need
being born of watered seed,

and I grow like twisted tree
having neither symmetry

nor the structure to avert
the falling axe, the minor hurt,

yet of one thing I am sure
that this bears my signature,

that I knew love when it came
and I called it by its name.

75

LOVE IS NOT ALL

EDNA ST. VINCENT MILLAY

Love is not all: it is not meat nor drink
Nor slumber nor a roof against the rain;
Nor yet a floating spar to men that sink
And rise and sink and rise and sink again;
Love can not fill the thickened lung with breath,
Nor clean the blood, nor set the fractured bone;
Yet many a man is making friends with death
Even as I speak, for lack of love alone.
It well may be that in a difficult hour,
Pinned down by pain and moaning for release,
Or nagged by want past resolution's power,
I might be driven to sell your love for peace,
Or trade the memory of this night for food.
It well may be. I do not think I would.

IF THOU MUST LOVE ME, LET IT BE FOR NOUGHT

ELIZABETH BARRETT BROWNING

If thou must love me, let it be for nought
Except for love's sake only. Do not say,
"I love her for her smile, her look, her way
Of speaking gently, for a trick of thought
That falls in well with mine, and certes brought
A sense of pleasant ease on such a day";
For these things in themselves, belovèd, may
Be changed, or change for thee: and love so wrought
May be unwrought so. Neither love me for
Thine own dear pity's wiping my cheeks dry:
A creature might forget to weep, who bore
Thy comfort long, and lose thy love thereby.
But love me for love's sake, that evermore
Thou mayst love on through love's eternity.

SONNET CXVI

WILLIAM SHAKESPEARE

Let me not to the marriage of true minds
Admit impediments. Love is not love
Which alters when it alteration finds,
Or bends with the remover to remove:
O no! it is an ever-fixèd mark
That looks on tempests, and is never shaken;
It is the star to every wandering bark,
Whose worth's unknown, although his height be taken.
Love's not Time's fool, though rosy lips and cheeks
Within his bending sickle's compass come;
Love alters not with his brief hours and weeks,
But bears it out ev'n to the edge of doom.
   If this be error, and upon me proved,
   I never writ, nor no man ever loved.

AGNES IN THE STROMNESS HOTEL

ROBERT LAWRENCE

As night mist settled on the shoulders of the island
I left the cobbled streets for the yellow warmth
of bar lights and peat smoke.

I asked at the counter if there was a local drink
and through your gin you told the woman tending bar
to serve me Scapa whisky.

Old at forty you asked where I was from.
Canada could have been Argyll or Africa,
they all meant far away and foreign

since young you married a neighbour's son
made sweaters and children
came to this pub each evening

and went down to the harbour
when nightly the sea
gave you back your man.

That night, between the female laughter,
smoke and spilled drinks,
we shared the world in each other's words.

I mouthed flat statements through the whisky
and you rolled stories onto the table
full of seas giving life and lashing the land

trees you planted torn from the earth by gales
and a son who went to fish;
a storm and body thrown onto the shore days later

identified by your pattern on the sweater.
Drink and talk passed until word came
the fishing boats were entering the harbour.

You stood, said goodbye
as if we would meet in this pub tomorrow
and walked into the night.

The bar emptied with you.
I finished my whisky alone;
watched a film of alcohol run down the glass.

With your words gathered off the table I climbed
the cliff above the harbour to watch
the boats come in and saw you

arms locked around your husband's neck.
Happy, the sea
had given him back again.

ABITATION

MARGARET ATWOOD

Marriage is not
a house or even a tent

it is before that, and colder:

the edge of the forest, the edge
of the desert
                the unpainted stairs
at the back where we squat
outside, eating popcorn

the edge of the receding glacier

where painfully and with wonder
at having survived even
this far

we are learning to make fire

5 THE LAST JOURNEY

THE POEMS

All things must pass

Because I Could Not Stop For Death/*Emily Dickinson* (USA 1830–1886)
The Term/*William Carlos Williams* (USA 1883–1963)
The Warner Bros./Shakespeare Hour/*Bert Almon* (Canada b. 1943)
Again and Again/*Earle Birney* (Canada b. 1904)

There is a pause

Small Miracles/*Joyce Carol Oates* (USA b. 1938)
The Last Journey/*Emma LaRocque* (Canada b. 1949)
The Mists at Asuka/*Yamabe Akahito* (Japan ?–c736 AD)

Life goes on

The Mill/*Richard Wilbur* (USA b. 1921)
Is my team ploughing/*A.E. Housman* (United Kingdom 1859–1936)
My Seven Deaths/*Joan Finnigan* (Canada b. 1925)

I am not resigned

Do Not Go Gentle Into That Good Night/*Dylan Thomas*
    (United Kingdom 1914–1953)
dying is fine) but death/*ee cummings* (USA 1894–1962)
Beside the Bed/*Charlotte Mew* (United Kingdom 1869–1928)
Dirge Without Music/*Edna St. Vincent Millay* (USA 1892–1950)

Part of the natural cycle

Post Humus/*Patti Tana* (USA)
Sowing/*Miguel Otero Silva* (Venezuela b. 1908)

We need not dread

Through All His Days His Jokes/*Joy Kogawa* (Canada b. 1935)
Death, Be Not Proud/*John Donne* (United Kingdom 1572?–1631)
The Coming of Winter/*Shirley Vogler Meister* (USA)
Song of the Traveller at Evening/*Johann Wolfgang von Goethe*
    (Germany 1749–1832)

BECAUSE I COULD NOT STOP FOR DEATH

EMILY DICKINSON

Because I could not stop for Death—
He kindly stopped for me—
The Carriage held but just Ourselves—
And Immortality.

We slowly drove—He knew no haste
And I had put away
My labor and my leisure too,
For His Civility—

We passed the School, where Children strove
At Recess—in the Ring—
We passed the Fields of Gazing Grain
We passed the Setting Sun—

Or rather—He passed Us—
The Dews drew quivering and chill—
For only Gossamer, my Gown—
My Tippet—only Tulle—

We paused before a House that seemed
A Swelling of the Ground—
The Roof was scarcely visible—
The Cornice—in the Ground—

Since then—'tis Centuries—and yet
Feels shorter than the Day
I first surmised the Horses Heads
Were toward Eternity—

THE TERM

WILLIAM CARLOS WILLIAMS

A rumpled sheet
of brown paper
about the length

and apparent bulk
of a man was
rolling with the

wind slowly over
and over in
the street as

a car drove down
upon it and
crushed it to

the ground. Unlike
a man it rose
again rolling

with the wind over
and over to be as
it was before.

THE WARNER BROS. / SHAKESPEARE HOUR

BERT ALMON

"Will you walk out of the air, my lord?"

The fine tuning won't prevent
channel 4 from drifting into 3
as a faint background
so that *Hamlet* is haunted
by ghostly figures
of the Coyote and the Roadrunner

As Hamlet says *"To be or not to be"*
I can make out the Coyote climbing
a ladder suspended in mid-air
Convention says he won't fall
until he tops the ladder and looks down
He'll smash on the desert floor
and come back renewed in another frame

Hamlet finishes his soliloquy
and greets the fair Ophelia
The Coyote has built a bomb
and lights the fuse
He has no trouble taking arms
while Hamlet is the man who looks down
and knows that resurrection
is not a convention of his play
We share his terror
rung by rung

AGAIN & AGAIN (1910)

EARL BIRNEY

That nightfall, when Dad rode back with mail,
he read us from the *Calgary Herald* about the comet.

"The weather's cleared. Moon down. After chores
let's all walk up the turnip hill and look for Halley."
"I've bread in the oven," Mother said. "You two go on,
and tell me later."

Alone above the dead-black woods we stared
into the blazing sky.
Near us an owl who-whoed.
I clung to my father's leathery hand.
There could be bears below.
"That's it!" he pointed, helped me find the haze
in the glittering millions.
A smudge with a streaky tail.
"Will it get lots bigger, Daddie?"
"Maybe, Buster. But remember it now, the way it is.
It won't be back till the nineteen-eighties!"

"It'll be bigger then," I said hopefully.
"And Mom will come and we'll all see it together."
"I'll long be dead when it's here again, son,
but you might live to see it."

I pulled my hand away, betrayed somehow.
"No, no. We'll see it together."
I knew some old people died, and cats, but not my Dad!
Not any of us. "We'll see Halley again, won't we? Dad?
Again and again?" His big hand circled mine once more,
but he didn't answer.

1986

$\mathcal{S}$MALL MIRACLES

JOYCE CAROL OATES

After the first death there is a shrinking.
Miracles to fit in a spoon.
The sun rolling free and crazy as the wheel of a baby buggy
      decades old.
The patchwork macaw in the children's zoo dipping
         its oversized beak up and down, up and down,
         merely to amuse.
The God of Trash flinging himself broken to the sidewalk.
The minutes that drain away noisily as we sleep.

Death?—but it was only a piercing, the fleeing
         thread through a needle's eye,
or the shy escape of steam that coalesces
on the first cold surface.

After the first death there is stillness.
The gaps of night between street lamps.
Hard-packed earth that turns to mud, and
         then to earth again, baked by the sun.
After the first death there is a pause.
And then the second death: a pause,
and the third.
This is what we have always known, but forget.

Is each subsequent death easier, one yearns to ask.

THE LAST JOURNEY

EMMA LaROCQUE

As expected
We threw pawfuls of earth on her casket
Wishing her well
As unexpected
The N.A.R. train whistled a farewell.
The loneliest, damned whistle I ever heard.

— — —

Train, blow a long, lonely whistle
When coming down the railroad tracks.
My mother won't be there
To meet you,
Waiting for her wayward children
At Mile 213, Chard.

86

THE MISTS AT ASUKA

V. AKAHITO
(Trans. Kenneth Rexroth)

The mists rise over
The still pools at Asuka.
Memory does not
Pass away so easily.

THE MILL

RICHARD WILBUR

The spoiling daylight inched along the bar-top,
Orange and cloudy, slowly igniting lint,
And then that glow was gone, and still your voice,
Serene with failure and with the ease of dying,
Rose from the shades that more and more became you.
Turning among its images, your mind
Produced the names of streets, the exact look
Of lilacs, 1903, in Cincinnati,
—Random, as if your testament were made,
The round sums all bestowed, and now you spent
Your pocket change, so as to be rid of it.
Or was it that you half-hoped to surprise
Your dead life's sound and sovereign anecdote?
What I remember best is the wrecked mill
You stumbled on in Tennessee; or was it
Somewhere down in Brazil? It slips my mind
Already. But there it was in a still valley
Far from the towns. No road or path came near it.
If there had been a clearing now it was gone,
And all you found amidst the choke of green
Was three walls standing, hurdled by great vines
And thatched by height on height of hushing leaves.
But still the mill-wheel turned! its crazy buckets
Creaking and lumbering out of the clogged race
And sounding, as you said, as if you'd found
Time all alone and talking to himself
In his eternal rattle.
                              How should I guess
Where they are gone to, now that you are gone,
Those fading streets and those most fragile lilacs,
Those fragmentary views, those times of day?
All that I can be sure of is the mill-wheel.
It turns and turns in my mind, over and over.

*I*S MY TEAM PLOUGHING

A.E. HOUSMAN

'Is my team ploughing,
  That I was used to drive
And hear and harness jingle
  When I was man alive?'

Ay, the horses trample,
  The harness jingles now;
No change though you lie under
  The land you used to plough.

'Is football playing
  Along the river shore,
With lads to chase the leather,
  Now I stand up no more?'

Ay, the ball is flying,
  The lads play heart and soul;
The goal stands up, the keeper
  Stands up to keep the goal.

'Is my girl happy,
  That I thought hard to leave,
And has she tired of weeping
  As she lies down at eve?'

Ay, she lies down lightly,
  She lies not down to weep:
Your girl is well contented.
  Be still, my lad, and sleep.

'Is my friend hearty,
  Now I am thin and pine,
And has he found to sleep in
  A better bed than mine?'

Yes, lad, I lie easy,
  I lie as lads would choose;
I cheer a dead man's sweetheart,
  Never ask me whose.

My Seven Deaths

JOAN FINNIGAN

When I was born the doctor said
to my father, "I think
we can save the mother,
but don't expect the child."

And I was born dead;

But the doctor
as some sort of experiment
or to add statistical data
to his paper on "Stubborn morbidity
in stillborns," maybe even
because I had an appealing quizzical look
on my face, the doctor
pounded me and flipped me in and out
of cold water and, after seven minutes,
straight from the collective unconscious
I gathered a bit of Old English
from Piers Plowman
and roared at the twentieth century.

When I was four I dabbled in death again;

I got Scarlet Fever
and, according the panic of those days,
was rushed to Isolation Hospital,
a Tender-Loving-Care-less place
of prunes and cascara;
once a week my parents could come
and wave to me through glass
and then they faded into another country;
from listening too intently
to my childhood deprivation,
Streptococci got into my ear;
the one-eyed ogre of a doctor came at me
with a midnight diagnosis,
"We must operate or it will hit the brain."
I screamed but they operated.
I think it hit the brain anyhow;
I have been writing poetry ever since.

And then there was the death of my First Love.

He said, "I've never loved you.
I just used you. Ha Ha."
And I got out of the car ready to die
on the sidewalk but the next morning,
after hot cocoa and a good cry,
I was angry enough to go on with the lessons.

Death came to me one summer's dawn in an aeroplane;

Yes, I actually talked face to face with him—
he isn't a bad sort really,
ugly but very straightforward and honest
about his objectives—
and after he showed me the hand he was holding
I moved from a jabbering chattering idiocy of fear
into a peace I made with myself,
wrapped my life into epitaph,

> "Here lies Joan aged twenty-one;
> She intended to stay longer."

When we landed I looked like
a purgatory saint, benign,
composed, beatific, my hands
touching the air,
and walking such unexpected steps
upon the earth.

At the birth of my first son
the surgeon made the emergency slit
that saved two. And I awoke to red roses
and the little damp beat-up ball
in my arms. All-Eyes we called him
because he had seen his first death
at birth.

At thirty-eight
there was a drowning that almost
dragged me under. I did everything
I could but refused the third demand.

Afterwards I paced the shores, the lanes,
the rooms, the streets,
cursing mothers and gods,
holding my drowned love in my arms again,
rescuing him in dream after dream
after dream.

That was the death that almost
took me down; before the event
I had unmasked symbiosis and I understood
the despairing music sucking me
downwards, downwards, over the edge,
madness demanding complement
even to the grave;
"You have one, but not two," I said
and clung to the Tree.

That was the death that slowed me;
I still dance but, if you know me well,
you sense the different quality,
the haunted pre-occupied air that strikes
without warning as though I was hearing
his death again, and resisting.

I am come here past seven deaths
to the promise of this sunny afternoon,
wind and bees in the basswoods,
blood summoned like sap
to the temples and the wrists

Tell me, my love, what deaths of yours
will deepen and darken these kisses?

DO NOT GO GENTLE INTO THAT GOOD NIGHT

DYLAN THOMAS

Do not go gentle into that good night,
Old age should burn and rave at close of day;
Rage, rage against the dying of the light.

Though wise men at their end know dark is right,
Because their words have forked no lightning they
Do not go gentle into that good night.

Good men, the last wave by, crying how bright
Their frail deeds might have danced in a green bay,
Rage, rage against the dying of the light.

Wild men who caught and sang the sun in flight,
And learn, too late, they grieved it on its way,
Do not go gentle into that good night.

Grave men, near death, who see with blinding sight
Blind eyes could blaze like meteors and be gay,
Rage, rage against the dying of the light.

And you, my father, there on the sad height,
Curse, bless, me now with your fierce tears, I pray.
Do not go gentle into that good night.
Rage, rage against the dying of the light.

DYING IS FINE)BUT DEATH

E. E. CUMMINGS

dying is fine)but death

?o
baby
i

wouldn't like

Death if Death
were
good:for

when(instead of stopping to think)you

begin to feel of it,dying
's miraculous
why?be

cause dying is

perfectly natural;perfectly
putting
it mildly lively(but

Death

is strictly
scientific
& artificial &
evil & legal)

we thank thee
god
almighty for dying

(forgive us,o life!the sin of Death

βESIDE THE BED

CHARLOTTE MEW

Someone has shut the shining eyes, straightened and folded
   The wandering hands quietly covering the unquiet breast:
So, smoothed and silenced you lie, like a child, not again to be questioned
               or scolded;
   But, for you, not one of us believes that this is rest.

Not so to close the windows down can cloud and deaden
   The blue beyond: or to screen the wavering flame subdue its breath:
Why, if I lay my cheek to your cheek, your grey lips, like dawn, would
               quiver and redden,
   Breaking into the old, odd smile at this fraud of death.

Because all night you have not turned to us or spoken
   It is time for you to wake; your dreams were never very deep:
I, for one, have seen the thin, bright, twisted threads of them dimmed
               suddenly and broken,
   This is only a most piteous pretence of sleep!

94

$\mathcal{D}$IRGE WITHOUT MUSIC

EDNA ST. VINCENT MILLAY

I am not resigned to the shutting away of loving hearts in
   the hard ground.
So it is, and so it will be, for so it has been, time out of
   mind:
Into the darkness they go, the wise and the lovely. Crowned
With lilies and with laurel they go; but I am not resigned.

Lovers and thinkers, into the earth with you.
Be one with the dull, the indiscriminate dust.
A fragment of what you felt, of what you knew,
A formula, a phrase remains,—but the best is lost.

The answers quick & keen, the honest look, the laughter,
    the love,
They are gone. They have gone to feed the roses. Elegant
    and curled
Is the blossom. Fragrant is the blossom. I know. But I do
    not approve.
More precious was the light in your eyes than all the roses
    in the world.

Down, down, down into the darkness of the grave
Gently they go, the beautiful, the tender, the kind;
Quietly they go, the intelligent, the witty, the brave.
I know. But I do not approve. And I am not resigned.

*P*OST HUMUS

PATTI TANA

Scatter my ashes in my garden
so I can be near my loves.
Say a few honest words, sing a gentle song,
join hands in a circle of flesh.
Please tell some stories about me
making you laugh. I love to make you laugh.
When I've had time to settle, and green
gathers into buds, remember I love blossoms
bursting in spring. As the season ripens
remember my persistent passion.
And if you come in my garden
on an August afternoon
pluck a bright red globe,
let juice run down your chin and the seeds
stick to your cheek. When I'm dead
I want folks to smile and say *That Patti,*
she sure is some tomato!

OWING

MIGUEL OTERO SILVA

When nothing remains of me but a tree,
when my bones have been scattered
beneath our mother earth:
when nothing remains of you but a white rose
nourished by that which once you were:
when the breath of the kiss that we exchange today
has embarked upon a thousand different breezes:
when even our names have become
mere sounds without echo
asleep in the shade of a fathomless sound:
then you will live on in the beauty of the rose,
and I in the rustling of the tree,
and our love in the murmur of the breeze.

Listen to me!
My wish for us is, to live
In the spoken words of men.
I would survive with you
in the deep lifestream of humanity:
in the laughter of children,
in the peace of mankind,
in love without weeping.

Therefore,
as we must give ourselves to the rose and the tree,
to the earth and the wind,
let us give ourselves, I beg you, to the future of the world.

THROUGH ALL HIS DAYS HIS JOKES

JOY KOGAWA

Through all his days his untimely jokes
were a stream of consciousness
constant spring thaw flooding into
any solemn or serious occasion.
Like summer in its exuberance uttering
flies, mosquitoes, zeppelin hornets
he would arrive with his harvest of cheer.
And here now at his autumn grave
the bird smiles, the grasshopper smiles
the tree sheds its leaves with
riotous shouting. All of earth
shares his mirth. "It's only
woolly winter I'm missing," he
says chuckling, "These untimely things
happen to us all."

DEATH, BE NOT PROUD

JOHN DONNE

Death, be not proud, though some have called thee
Mighty and dreadful, for thou art not so;
For those whom thou think'st thou dost overthrow
Die not, poor Death, nor yet canst thou kill me.
From rest and sleep, which but thy pictures be,
Much pleasure, then from thee much more must flow,
And soonest our best men with thee do go,
Rest of their bones, and soul's delivery.
Thou art slave to fate, chance, kings, and desperate men,
And dost with poison, war, and sickness dwell,
And poppy or charms can make us sleep as well,
And better than thy stroke; why swell'st thou then?
One short sleep past, we wake eternally,
And death shall be no more; Death, thou shalt die.

THE COMING OF WINTER

SHIRLEY VOGLER MEISTER

The winter winds have chilled the warmth we knew
and whirl our unmet dreams like crumbling leaves
around the barren trees: a rendezvous
of weathered bones and somber dance which weaves
despair with sparks of hope that summon spring.
Beyond the wailing wind is sanguine sound—
the vigor-voice that wakes all slumbering—
the reassuring call of power more profound.
We acquiesce to freezing winds and test
our mettle 'gainst the spectral storms ahead,
for there are forces that we can't arrest
and states of nature that we need not dread.
Beyond the winds lie gentler joys and peace
that sanctify our fate and death's caprice.

SONG OF THE TRAVELLER
AT EVENING

JOHANN WOLFGANG von GOETHE

Over all the hills now,
Repose.
In all the trees now
Shows
Barely a breath. Birds are through
That rang in their wood to the west.
Only wait, traveller. Rest
Soon for you too.

6 *B*ROKEN IMAGES

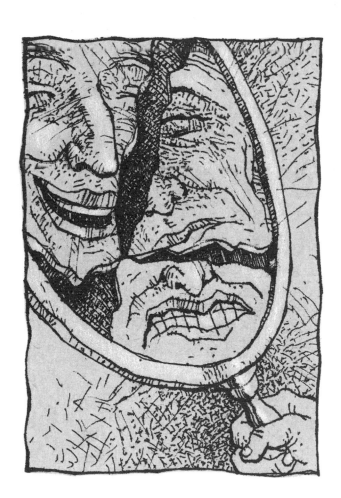

THE POEMS

Fear and doubt

Fear and Doubt/*Erich Fried* (Germany b. 1921)
In Broken Images/*Robert Graves* (United Kingdom 1895–1985)
Provisions/*Margaret Atwood* (Canada b. 1939)

Fearful symmetry

The Tyger/*William Blake* (United Kingdom 1757–1827)
Mirror/*John Updike* (USA b. 1932)

Fate intervenes

I would not be here . . ./*John Hartford* (USA b. 1937)
To a Mouse/*Robert Burns* (United Kingdom 1759–1796)
The Man He Killed/*Thomas Hardy* (United Kingdom 1840–1928)
Auto Wreck/*Karl Shapiro* (USA)

Through purblind night

Here/*Octavio Paz* (Mexico b. 1914)
Patterns/*Paul Simon* (USA b. 1942)
The Wiper/*Louis MacNiece* (United Kingdom 1907–1963)

Nothing to do but wait

The Second Coming/*W.B. Yeats* (Ireland 1865–1939)
The Great Wall/*Patrick Lane* (Canada b. 1939)
Waiting for the Barbarians/*Constantine P. Cavafy* (Greece 1863–1933)

Even in the darkest hour

Dover Beach/*Matthew Arnold* (United Kingdom 1822–1888)
On his blindness/*John Milton* (United Kingdom 1608–1674)
The Largest Life/*Archibald Lampman* (Canada 1861–1899)

ℱEAR AND DOUBT

ERICH FRIED

do not doubt
the man
who tells you
he's afraid

but be afraid
of the man
who tells you
he never doubts

1974: Gegengift

ℐN BROKEN IMAGES

ROBERT GRAVES

He is quick, thinking in clear images;
I am slow, thinking in broken images.

He becomes dull, trusting to his clear images;
I become sharp, mistrusting my broken images.

Trusting his images, he assumes their relevance;
Mistrusting my images, I question their relevance.

Assuming their relevance, he assumes the fact;
Questioning their relevance, I question the fact.

When the fact fails him, he questions his senses;
When the fact fails me, I approve my senses.

He continues quick and dull in his clear images;
I continue slow and sharp in my broken images.

He in a new confusion of his understanding;
I in a new understanding of my confusion.

*ρ*ROVISIONS

MARGARET ATWOOD

What should we have taken
with us? We never could decide
on that; or what to wear,
or at what time of
year we should make this journey

so here we are, in thin
raincoats and rubber boots

on the disastrous ice, the wind rising,

nothing in our pockets

but a pencil stub, two oranges
four toronto streetcar tickets

and an elastic band, holding a bundle
of small white filing-cards
printed with important facts.

THE TYGER

WILLIAM BLAKE

Tyger! Tyger! burning bright
In the forests of the night,
What immortal hand or eye
Could frame thy fearful symmetry?

In what distant deeps or skies
Burnt the fire of thine eyes?
On what wings dare he aspire?
What the hand dare seize the fire?

And what shoulder, & what art,
Could twist the sinews of thy heart?
And when thy heart began to beat,
What dread hand? & what dread feet?

What the hammer? what the chain?
In what furnace was thy brain?
What the anvil? what dread grasp
Dare its deadly terrors clasp?

When the stars threw down their spears,
And water'd heaven with their tears,
Did he smile his work to see?
Did he who made the Lamb make thee?

Tyger! Tyger! burning bright
In the forests of the night,
What immortal hand or eye,
Dare frame thy fearful symmetry?

MIRROR

JOHN UPDIKE

104

When you look
into a mirror
it is not
yourself you see,
but a kind
of apish error
posed in fearful
symmetry.

I WOULD NOT BE HERE

JOHN HARTFORD

I would not be here
If I hadn't been there
I wouldn't been there
if I hadn't just turned
on Wednesday the third
in the late afternoon
got to talking with George
who works out in the back
and only because
he was getting off early
to go see a man
at a Baker Street bookstore
with a rare first edition
of steamboats and cotton
a book he would never
have sought in the first place
had he not been inspired
by a fifth grade replacement
school teacher in Kirkwood
who was picked just at random
by some man on a school board
who couldn't care less
and she wouldn't been working
if not for her husband
who moved two months prior
to work in the office
of a man he had met
while he served in the army
and only because
they were in the same barracks
an accident caused

by a poorly made roster
mixed up on the desk
of a sergeant from Denver
who wouldn't be in
but for being in back
in a car he was riding
before he enlisted
that hit a cement truck
and killed both his buddies
but a back seat flew up there
and spared him from dying
and only because
of the fault of a workman
who forgot to turn screws
on a line up in Detroit
'cause he hollered at Sam
who was hateful that morning
hung over from drinking
alone at a tavern
because of a woman
he wished he'd not married
he met long ago
at a Jewish bar mitzvah
for the son of a man
who had moved there from Jersey
who managed the drugstore
that sold the prescription
that cured up the illness
he caught way last summer
he wouldn't have caught
except . . .

105

To a Mouse

ROBERT BURNS

ON TURNING HER UP IN HER NEST WITH THE PLOUGH,
NOVEMBER 1785

Wee, sleekit, cowran, tim'rous beastie,
Oh, what a panic's in thy breastie !
Thou need na start awa sae hasty,
    Wi' bickering brattle !
I wad be laith to rin an' chase thee,
    Wi' murd'ring pattle !

I'm truly sorry man's dominion
Has broken nature's social union,
An' justifies that ill opinion
    Which makes thee startle
At me, thy poor earth-born companion,
    An' fellow-mortal !

I doubt na, whyles, but thou may thieve ;
What then ? poor beastie, thou maun live !
A daimen icker in a thrave
    'S a sma' request :
I'll get a blessin wi' the lave,
    And never miss't !

Thy wee bit housie, too, in ruin !
It's silly wa's the win's are strewin' !
An' naething, now, to big a new ane,
    O' foggage green !
An' bleak December's winds ensuin,
    Baith snell and keen !

Thou saw the fields laid bare an' waste,
An' weary winter comin fast,
An' cozie here, beneath the blast,
    Thou thought to dwell,
'Till crash ! the cruel coulter past
    Out thro' thy cell.

That wee bit heap o' leaves an' stibble
Has cost thee mony a weary nibble !
Now thou's turn'd out, for a' thy trouble,
        But house or hald,
To thole the winter's sleety dribble,
        An' cranreuch cauld !

But, Mousie, thou art no thy lane,
In proving foresight may be vain :
The best laid schemes o' mice an' men,
        Gang aft agley,
An' lea'e us nought but grief and pain,
        For promis'd joy !

Still, thou art blest, compar'd wi' me !
The present only toucheth thee :
But, och ! I backward cast my ee,
        On prospects drear !
An' forward, tho' I canna see,
        I guess an' fear !

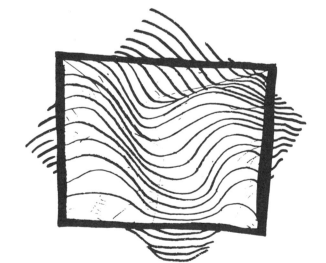

THE MAN HE KILLED

THOMAS HARDY

Had he and I but met
  By some old ancient inn,
We should have sat us down to wet
  Right many a nipperkin!

But ranged as infantry,
  And staring face to face,
I shot at him as he at me,
  And killed him in his place.

I shot him dead because—
  Because he was my foe,
Just so: my foe of course he was;
  That's clear enough; although

He thought he'd 'list, perhaps
  Off-hand-like—just as I—
Was out of work—had sold his traps—
  No other reason why.

Yes; quaint and curious war is!
  You shoot a fellow down
You'd treat if met where any bar is,
  Or help to half-a-crown.

108

Auto Wreck

KARL SHAPIRO

Its quick soft silver bell beating, beating,
And down the dark one ruby flare
Pulsing out red like an artery,
The ambulance at top speed floating down
Past beacons and illuminated clocks
Wings in a heavy curve, dips down
And brakes speed, entering the crowd.
The doors leap open, emptying light;
Stretchers are laid out, the mangled lifted
And stowed into the little hospital.
Then the bell, breaking the hush, tolls once,
And the ambulance with its terrible cargo
Rocking, slightly rocking, moves away,
As the doors, an afterthought, are closed.

We are deranged,walking among the cops
Who sweep glass and are large and composed.
One is still making notes under the light.
One with a bucket douches ponds of blood
Into the street and gutter.
One hangs lanterns on the wrecks that cling,
Empty husks of locusts, to iron poles.

Our throats were tight as tourniquets,
Our feet were bound with splints, but now,
Like convalescents intimate and gauche,
We speak through sickly smiles and warn
With the stubborn saw of common sense,
The grim joke and the banal resolution.
The traffic moves around with care,
But we remain, touching a wound
That opens to our richest horror.

Already old, the question Who shall die?
Becomes unspoken Who is innocent?
For death in war is done by hands;
Suicide has cause and stillbirth, logic;
And cancer, simple as a flower, blooms.
But this invites the occult mind,
Cancels our physics with a sneer,
And spatters all we knew of denouement
Across the wicked and expedient stones.

 # HERE

OCTAVIO PAZ

My footsteps in this street
Re-echo
      In another street
Where
     I hear my footsteps
Passing in this street
Where

Nothing is real but the fog

 # PATTERNS

PAUL SIMON

The night sets softly with the hush of falling leaves.
Casting shivering shadows on the houses through the trees.
And the light from the street lamp makes a pattern on my wall,
Like the pieces of a puzzle or a child's uneven scrawl.

Up a narrow flight of stairs in a narrow little room,
As I lie upon my bed in the early evening gloom,
Impaled on my wall my eyes can dimly see
The pattern of my life and the puzzle that is me.

From the moment of my birth to the instant of my death,
There are patterns I must follow just as I must breathe each breath.
Like a rat in a maze the path before me lies,
And the pattern never alters until the rat dies.

The pattern still remains on the wall where darkness fell,
And it's fitting that it should for in darkness I must dwell.
Like the color of my skin or the day that I grow old,
My life is made of patterns that can scarcely be controlled.

THE WIPER

LOUIS MacNEICE

Through purblind night the wiper
Reaps a swathe of water
On the screen; we shudder on
   And hardly hold the road,
All we can see a segment
Of blackly shining asphalt
With the wiper moving across it
   Clearing, blurring, clearing.

But what to say of the road?
The monotony of its hardly
Visible camber, the mystery
   Of its far invisible margins,
Will these be always with us,
The night being broken only
By lights that pass or meet us
   From others in moving boxes?

Boxes of glass and water
Upholstered, equipped with dials
Professing to tell the distance
   We have gone, the speed we are
     going,
But never a gauge nor needle
To tell us where we are going
Or when day will come, supposing
   This road exists in daytime.

For now we cannot remember
Where we were when it was not
Night, when it was not raining,
   Before this car moved forward
And the wiper backward and forward
Lighting so little before us
Of a road that, crouching forward,
   We watch move always towards us,

Which through the tiny segment
Cleared and blurred by the wiper
Is sucked in under the axle
    To be spewed behind us and lost
While we, dazzled by darkness,
Haul the black future towards us
Peeling the skin from our hands;
    And yet we hold the road.

THE SECOND COMING

WILLIAM BUTLER YEATS

Turning and turning in the widening gyre
The falcon cannot hear the falconer;
Things fall apart, the centre cannot hold;
Mere anarchy is loosed upon the world,
The blood-dimmed tide is loosed, and everywhere
The ceremony of innocence is drowned;
The best lack of all conviction, while the worst
Are full of passionate intensity.

Surely some revelation is at hand;
Surely the Second Coming is at hand;
The Second Coming! Hardly are those words out
When a vast image out of *Spiritus Mundi*
Troubles my sight: somewhere in sands of the desert
A shape with lion body and the head of a man,
A gaze blank and pitiless as the sun,
Is moving its slow thighs, while all about it
Reel shadows of the indignant desert birds.
The darkness drops again, but now I know
That twenty centuries of stony sleep
Were vexed to nightmare by a rocking cradle,
And what rough beast, its hour come round at last,
Slouches towards Bethlehem to be born?

THE GREAT WALL

PATRICK LANE

There is a moment on the wall when a man looks out
over the far horizon and wonders when
they will come. He does not know who they are.
The wall was built many years ago, long
before he was born and before his father was
born. All his life has been spent
repairing the wall, replacing the fallen
stones, clearing away the tough grass
that grows like fingers in the masonry.

Inside the wall the land is the same
as outside and once, when he was confused
by the hot wind, he could not remember
which side of the wall he lived on and he
has never forgotten the doubt of that day.
He has seen no one but his family for years.
They were given this work by someone
a long time ago or so his father said
but who it was he did not remember,
it was before his time.

But there comes a moment, there always does,
when a man stops his work, lays down his tools,
looks out over the dry brown distance
and wonders when they will come, the ones
the wall is meant for. At that moment
he sees between earth and sky
a cloud of dust like the drifting spores
of a puffball exploded by a foot.

He knows there is nothing to do but wait,
nothing he can do but stand on the wall. Everything
is in order, the wall as perfect as a man
can make it. It does not occur to him
that the cloud might be only a cloud of dust,
something the wind has raised out of nothing
and which will return to nothing. For a moment
he wonders what will happen when they come.
Will they honour him for his work, the hours
and years he has spent? But which side
of the wall do they come from?
No one has ever told him what would happen.

He will have to tell his son, he thinks,
his wife. He wishes his father were alive
to see them coming, but he is not,
and his son, who has already learned
the secrets of stone, is asleep.
It is a day to remember.
In all his life he has never been more
afraid, he has never been happier.

$\mathcal{W}$AITING FOR THE BARBARIANS

CONSTANTINE P. CAVAFY

What are we waiting for, assembled in the forum?

    The barbarians are due here today.

Why isn't anything going on in the senate?
Why are the senators sitting there without legislating?

    Because the barbarians are coming today.
    What's the point of senators making laws now?
    Once the barbarians are here, they'll do the legislating.

Why did our emperor get up so early,
and why is he sitting enthroned at the city's main gate,
in state, wearing the crown?

    Because the barbarians are coming today
    and the emperor's waiting to receive their leader.
    He's even got a scroll to give him,
    loaded with titles, with imposing names.

Why have our two consuls and praetors come out today
wearing their embroidered, their scarlet togas?
Why have they put on bracelets with so many amethysts,
rings sparkling with magnificent emeralds?
Why are they carrying elegant canes
beautifully worked in silver and gold?

    Because the barbarians are coming today
    and things like that dazzle the barbarians.

Why don't our distinguished orators turn up as usual
to make their speeches, say what they have to say?

    Because the barbarians are coming today
    and they're bored by rhetoric and public speaking.

Why this sudden bewilderment, this confusion?
(How serious people's faces have become.)
Why are the streets and squares emptying so rapidly,
everyone going home lost in thought?

    Because night has fallen and the barbarians haven't come.
    And some of our men just in from the border say
    there are no barbarians any longer.

Now what's going to happen to us without barbarians?
Those people were a kind of solution.

OVER BEACH

MATTHEW ARNOLD

The sea is calm to-night.
The tide is full, the moon lies fair
Upon the straits; —on the French coast the light
Gleams and is gone; the cliffs of England stand,
Glimmering and vast, out in the tranquil bay.
Come to the window, sweet is the night-air!
Only, from the long line of spray
Where the sea meets the moon-blanch'd sand,
Listen! You hear the grating roar
Of pebbles which the waves draw back, and fling,
At their return, up the high strand,
Begin, and cease, and then again begin,
With tremulous cadence slow, and bring
The eternal note of sadness in.

Sophocles long ago
Heard it on the Ægean, and it brought
Into his mind the turbid ebb and flow
Of human misery; we
Find also in the sound a thought,
Hearing it by this distant northern sea.

The sea of faith
Was once, too, at the full, and round earth's shore
Lay like the folds of a bright girdle furl'd.
But now I only hear
Its melancholy, long, withdrawing roar.
Retreating, to the breath
Of the night-wind, down the vast edges drear
And naked shingles of the world.

Ah, love, let us be true
To one another! for the world, which seems
To lie before us like a land of dreams,
So various, so beautiful, so new,
Hath really neither joy, nor love, nor light,
Nor certitude, nor peace, nor help for pain;
And we are here as on a darkling plain
Swept with confused alarms of struggle and flight,
Where ignorant armies clash by night.

ON HIS BLINDNESS

JOHN MILTON

When I consider how my light is spent,
    Ere half my days, in this dark world and wide,
    And that one Talent which is death to hide,
    Lodg'd with me useless, though my Soul more bent
To serve therewith my Maker, and present
    My true account, least he returning chide,
    Doth God exact day-labour, light deny'd,
    I fondly ask; But patience to prevent
That murmur, soon replies, God doth not need
    Either man's work or his own gifts, who best
    Bear his milde yoak, they serve him best, his State
Is Kingly. Thousands at his bidding speed
    And post o're Land and Ocean without rest:
    They also serve who only stand and waite.

THE LARGEST LIFE

ARCHIBALD LAMPMAN

There is a beauty at the goal of life,
A beauty growing since the world began,
Through every age and race, through lapse and strife,
Till the great human soul completes her span.
Beneath the waves of storm that lash and burn,
The currents of blind passion that appal,
To listen and keep watch till we discern
The tide of sovereign truth that guides it all;
So to address our spirits to the height,
And so attune them to the valiant whole,
That the great light be greater for our light,
And the great soul the stronger for our soul:
To have done this is to have lived, though fame
Remember us with no familiar name.

7 PLAYING THE FOOL

THE POEMS

*P*LAYS

WALTER SAVAGE LANDOR

Alas, how soon the hours are over,
Counted us out to play the lover!—
And how much narrower is the stage,
Allotted us to play the sage!
But when we play the fool, how wide
The theatre expands! beside,
How long the audience sits before us!
How many prompters! what a chorus!

*E*XPERIENCE TO LET

OGDEN NASH

Experience is a futile teacher,
Experience is a prosy preacher,
Experience is a fruit tree fruitless,
Experience is a shoe-tree bootless.
For sterile wearience and drearience,
Depend, my boy, upon experience.
The burnt child, urged by rankling ire,
Can hardly wait to get back at the fire.
And, mulcted in the gambling den,
Men stand in line to gamble again.
Who says that he can drink or not?
The sober man? Nay nay, the sot.
He who has never tasted jail
Lives well within the legal pale,
While he who's served a heavy sentence
Renews the racket, not repentance.
The nation bankrupt by a war
Thinks to recoup with just one more;
The wretched golfer, divot-bound,
Persists in dreams of the perfect round;
Life's little suckers chirp like crickets
While spending their all on losing tickets.

People whose instinct instructs them naught,
But must by experience be taught,
Will never learn by suffering once,
But ever and ever play the dunce.
Experience! Wise men do not need it!
Experience! Idiots do not heed it!
I'd trade my lake of experience
For just one drop of common sense.

ELL ALL THE TRUTH

EMILY DICKINSON

Tell all the truth but tell it slant,
Success in circuit lies,
Too bright for our infirm delight
The truth's superb surprise,

As lightning to the children eased
With explanation kind,
The truth must dazzle gradually
Or every man be blind.

TH TOMATO CONSPIRACY AINT WORTH A WHOL POME

BILL BISSETT

          very few peopul
   realize ths but altho yu have 5 or 6
billyun peopul walking around beleeving

that tomatoez ar red   they ar
    actually blu   nd ar sprayd
red to make ther apperance
   consistent with peopuls beleef

    i was whuns inside th
   largest tomato spraying plant
in th world with binoculars nd
   camoflage material all ovr me

     nd ive got th pictures to proov it
   oranges uv corz ar not orange nor ar lemons
    lemon color   its all a marage   it

was decreed what color things
   wud b at th beginning nd then
     theyve bin colord that
       way evr since

      it adds to th
   chemcials nd artifishulness uv everything
we eet tho did yu know that oranges
   ar actually a discouraging off
   color

   i was luky really to get
out uv th tomato factoree alive
   th tomatoez wer really
     upset to b xposd

*C*ALAMITY

F.R. SCOTT

A laundry truck
Rolled down the hill
And crashed into my maple tree.
It was a truly North American calamity.
Three cans of beer fell out
(Which in itself was revealing)
And a jumble of skirts and shirts
Spilled onto the ploughed grass.
Dogs barked, and the children
Sprouted like dandelions on my lawn.
Normally we do not speak to one another on this avenue,
But the excitement made us suddenly neighbours.
People exchanged remarks
Who had never been introduced
And for a while we were quite human.
Then the policeman came—
Sedately, for this was Westmount—
And carefully took down all names and numbers.
The towing truck soon followed,
Order was restored.
The starch came raining down.

*M*ENDING WALL

ROBERT FROST

Something there is that doesn't love a wall,
That sends the frozen-ground-swell under it,
And spills the upper boulders in the sun,
And makes gaps even two can pass abreast.
The work of hunters is another thing:
I have come after them and made repair
Where they have left not one stone on a stone,
But they would have the rabbit out of hiding,
To please the yelping dogs. The gaps I mean,

No one has seen them made or heard them made,
But at spring mending-time we find them there.
I let my neighbor know beyond the hill;
And on a day we meet to walk the line
And set the wall between us once again.
We keep the wall between us as we go.
To each the boulders that have fallen to each.
And some are loaves and some so nearly balls
We have to use a spell to make them balance:
"Stay where you are until our backs are turned!"
We wear our fingers rough with handling them.
Oh, just another kind of outdoor game,
One on a side. It comes to little more:
There where it is we do not need the wall:
He is all pine and I am apple orchard.
My apple trees will never get across
And eat the cones under his pines, I tell him.
He only says, "Good fences make good neighbors."
Spring is the mischief in me, and I wonder
If I could put a notion in his head:
"*Why* do they make good neighbors? Isn't it
Where there are cows? But here there are no cows.
Before I built a wall I'd ask to know
What I was walling in or walling out,
And to whom I was like to give offence.
Something there is that doesn't love a wall,
That wants it down." I could say "Elves" to him,
But it's not elves exactly, and I'd rather
He said it for himself. I see him there
Bringing a stone grasped firmly by the top
In each hand, like an old-stone savage armed.
He moves in darkness as it seems to me,
Not of woods only and the shade of trees.
He will not go behind his father's saying,
And he likes having thought of it so well
He says again, "Good fences make good neighbors."

THE HEN AND THE ORIOLE

DON MARQUIS

well boss did it
ever strike you that a
hen regrets it just as
much when they wring her
neck as an oriole but
nobody has any
sympathy for a hen because
she is not beautiful
while every one gets
sentimental over the
oriole and says how
shocking to kill the
lovely thing this thought
comes to my mind
because of the earnest
endeavor of a
gentleman to squash me
yesterday afternoon when i
was riding up in the
elevator if i had been a
butterfly he would have
said how did that
beautiful thing happen to
find its way into
these grimy city streets do
not harm the splendid
creature but let it
fly back to its rural
haunts again beauty always
gets the best of
it be beautiful boss
a thing of beauty is a
joy forever
be handsome boss and let
who will be clever is
the sad advice
of your ugly little friend
                    archy

SOMETHING OF VALUE

MARYA MANNES

"Thieves Nonplussed.
Enter Abstract Art Gallery
But Leave Empty-Handed."

Behold the fate of the poor thief
Who comes unwittingly to grief,
And conquers the obstructive lock
Only to find himself in shock,
Seized by alarm and then displeasure
At finding trash instead of treasure.
Or so he thinks, the wretched fool,
Untutored in the Abstract school,
For what he left behind in haste
Was treasure to the tutored taste,
And, quite the contrary from trash,
Could be converted into cash.

PUBLIC AID FOR NIAGARA FALLS

MORRIS BISHOP

Upon the patch of earth that clings
   Near the very brink of doom,
Where the frenzied water flings
   Downward to a misty gloom,

Where the earth in terror quakes
   And the water leaps in foam
Plunging, frantic, from the Lakes,
   Hurrying seaward, hurrying home,

Where Man's little voice is vain,
   And his heart chills in his breast
At the dreadful yell of pain
   Of the waters seeking rest;

There I stood, and humbly scanned
   The miracle that sense appalls,
And I watched the tourist stand
   Spitting in Niagara Falls.

$\mathcal{S}$UBSTITUTE

SHIRLEY I. PAUSTIAN

Quadratic functions
Is what it says at the top of the page.
Except for the sniffles of the boy in the front desk
The room is quiet.
Do you offer grade twelve a Kleenex?

The math teacher left a test.
Equations—yes—but what is a vertex?
And where did a and b come from?
Once I would have known.

No. 69,
Second from the back in the third row,
Squirms and watches me.
He steals a furtive glance at the paper across
    the aisle.
No help there; the blind leads the blind.

The farmer's oats increases in yield by three bushels
    a day,
And the price falls at a prescribed daily rate.
Draw the graph.
When should the farmer sell?
Farm kids would say, suppose it hails? or snows?
What about shelling? Grasshoppers? And who says
That prices will go down?
City kids, these.

The girl in front of 69 moves to one side.
He stretches his neck, peers anxiously, turns back
    a page
And writes.
The kinky-haired kid with the grin is finished.
Can I go now?
Can't you find something useful to do here?
Me? Useful? The grin widens. You gotta be kiddin!
He'll get by.

It's the 69's I worry about.
Stand on your own feet, kid;
Take your licks.
The world forgives the honest grin,
But the shifty eye
Opens no pathways.

WAYMAN IN THE WORKFORCE: ACTIVELY SEEKING EMPLOYMENT

TOM WAYMAN

Everybody was very nice. Each place Wayman went
the receptionist said: "Certainly we are hiring.
Just fill out one of these forms." Then, silence.
Wayman would call back each plant and corporation
and his telephone would explain: "Well, you see,
we do our hiring pretty much at random. Our interviewers
draw someone out of the stack of applications we have on file.
There's no telling when you might be notified: could be next week
or the week after that. Or, you might never hear from us at all."

One Thursday afternoon, Wayman's luck ran out.
He had just completed a form for a motor truck
manufacturing establishment, handed it in to the switchboard
    operator
and was headed happily out. "Just a minute, sir," the girl said.
"Please take a seat over there. Someone will see you about this."

Wayman's heart sank. He heard her dialling Personnel.
"There's a guy here willing to work full time
and he says he'll do anything," she said excitedly.
Around the corner strode a man in a suit. "Want a job, eh?" he said.
He initialled one corner of the application and left.
Then a man in a white coat appeared. "I'm Gerry," the newcomer said.
"This way." And he was gone through a doorway into the plant.

"We make seven trucks a day," Gerry shouted
standing sure-footedly amid a clanking, howling, bustling din.
"Over here is the cab shop, where you'll work. I'll be your foreman.
And here is the chassis assembly . . ." a speeding forklift narrowly
    missed them
" . . . and this is where we make the parts."
"Wait a minute," Wayman protested, his voice barely audible
above the roar of hammers, drills, and the rivet guns. "I'm pretty green
at this sort of thing."

                        "Nothing to worry about," Gerry said.
"Can you start tomorrow? Monday? Okay,
you enter through this door. I'll meet you here."
They were standing near an office marked *First Aid*.
"We have to do a minor physical on you now," Gerry said.
"Just step inside. I'll see you Monday."

Wayman went shakily in through the First Aid office doors.
"I need your medical history," the attendant said
as Wayman explained who he was. "Stand over here.
Thank you. Now drop your pants."
Wayman did as he was told. "You seem sort of nervous to me,"
the aid man said, as we wrote down notes to himself.
"Me, I'm a bit of an amateur psychologist. There are 500 men
in this plant, and I know 'em all.
Got to, in my job. You shouldn't be nervous.
Remember when you apply for work you're really selling yourself.
Be bold. Where are you placed? Cab shop?
Nothing to worry about working there: monkey see, monkey do."

Then Wayman was pronounced fit, and the aid man escorted him
back through the roaring maze into the calm offices of Personnel.
There Wayman had to sign for time cards, employee number, health
    scheme
and only just managed to decline
company credit union, company insurance plan, and a company
    social club.
At last he was released, and found himself back on the street
clutching his new company parking lot sticker in a light rain.
Even in his slightly dazed condition,
a weekend away from actually starting work, Wayman could tell
he had just been hired.

✐HE MILLER

GEOFFREY CHAUCER
(Trans. Nevil Coghill)

from The Canterbury Tales

      The Miller was a chap of sixteen stone,
A great stout fellow big in brawn and bone.
He did well out of them, for he could go
And win the ram at any wrestling show.
Broad, knotty and short-shouldered, he would boast
He could heave any door off hinge and post,
Or take a run and break it with his head.
His beard, like any sow or fox, was red
And broad as well, as though it were a spade;
And, at its very tip, his nose displayed
A wart on which there stood a tuft of hair
Red as the bristles in an old sow's ear.
His nostrils were as black as they were wide,
He had a sword and a buckler at his side,
His mighty mouth was like a furnace door.
A wrangler and buffoon, he had a store
Of tavern stories, filthy in the main.
His was a master-hand at stealing grain.
He felt it with this thumb and thus he knew
Its quality and took three times his due—
A thumb of gold, by God, to gauge an oat!
He wore a hood of blue and a white coat.
He liked to play his bagpipes up and down
And that was how he brought us out of town.

131

*I*N WESTMINSTER ABBEY

JOHN BETJEMAN

Let me take this other glove off
  As the *vox humana* swells,
And the beauteous fields of Eden
  Bask beneath the Abbey bells.
Here, where England's statesmen lie,
Listen to a lady's cry.

Gracious Lord, oh bomb the Germans.
  Spare their women for Thy Sake,
And if that is not too easy
  We will pardon Thy Mistake.
But, gracious Lord, whate'er shall be,
Don't let anyone bomb me.

Keep our Empire undismembered
  Guide our Forces by Thy Hand,
Gallant blacks from far Jamaica,
  Honduras and Togoland;
Protect them Lord in all their fights,
And, even more, protect the whites.

Think of what our Nation stands for,
  Books from Boots' and country lanes,
Free speech, free passes, class distinction,
  Democracy and proper drains.
Lord, put beneath Thy special care
One-eighty-nine Cadogan Square.

Although dear Lord I am a sinner,
  I have done no major crime;
Now I'll come to Evening Service
  Whensoever I have time.
So, Lord, reserve for me a crown,
And do not let my shares go down.

I will labour for Thy Kingdom,
  Help our lads to win the war,
Send white feathers to the cowards,
  Join the Women's Army Corps,
Then wash the Steps around Thy Throne
In the Eternal Safety Zone.

132

Now I feel a little better,
　　What a treat to hear Thy Word,
Where the bones of leading statesmen,
　　Have so often been interred.
And now, dear Lord, I cannot wait
Because I have a luncheon date.

DANIEL AT BREAKFAST

PHYLLIS McGINLEY

His paper propped against the electric toaster
　　(Nicely adjusted to his morning use),
Daniel at breakfast studies world disaster
　　And sips his orange juice.

The words dismay him. Headlines shrilly chatter
　　Of famine, storm, death, pestilence, decay.
Daniel is gloomy, reaching for the butter.
　　He shudders at the way

War stalks the planet still, and men know hunger,
　　Go shelterless, betrayed, may perish soon.
The coffee's weak again. In sudden anger
　　Daniel throws down his spoon

And broods a moment on the kitchen faucet
　　The plumber mended, but has mended ill;
Recalls tomorrow means a dental visit,
　　Laments the grocery bill.

Then, having shifted from his human shoulder
　　The universal woe, he drains his cup,
Rebukes the weather (surely turning colder),
　　Crumples his napkin up
And, kissing his wife abruptly at the door,
Stamps fiercely off to catch the 8:04.

THE SICK DEER

JOAN FINNIGAN

Four men in the Gatineau Hills,
ski-ing along the dazzling trails of March,
found a sick deer
    lying helpless
      in the snow.

The fallen animal raised its head
and turned on them
the gentle pleading pools of those eyes
which only fail to move killers,

and it cried like something human,
and tried to rise
but fell back

the four skiers stood in a semi-circle
as stricken as men

faced with a woman in tears
and the first of them bent down
and gathered the sick animal

into his arms and they began,
by mutual consent,
a long Samaritan journey
back to civilization.

the deer was a yearling;
it weighted forty-five pounds
and they had to take turns
carrying the burden of their humanity,
down the steep hills,
across the long trails.

flagging, stumbling, sweating,
two of them remembering the weight of wounded buddies
at Salerno and Dieppe,
they made the long trek back over the miles
with the sick deer in their arms,
collecting a retinue of skiers
as they came out of the wilderness
into the areas
crawling with human hill-flies.

at the first Aid outpost
the crowds gathered around;
the tow ran alone,
a caesura in pleasure,
and many eyes watched the Night Rider
and the four committed men
wrap the sick deer in blankets
and strap him in a toboggan
for the last stretch of the journey
down to the road.

there was not enough all people joined together
could do for that sick deer;
many offered help;
others kept their longings to themselves
and one woman said,
in a voice that reeled through the hills,
"Oh, isn't it terrible,
    it cries
        just like a child."

at the road they tucked the shivering animal
into the back seat of one of their cars
and drove with a real sense of emergency
to a veterinarian in Hull
who, without question of fee,
used all his equipment and skill
to treat the creature
which died a few hours later
       of a mysterious undiagnosed disease.

back in the hills,
the tows resumed full speed,
sucked into their clanging maws
a whole long line after line
of impatient humans
and spewed them all out
at the tops of hills
never into the dusk done with the obsessive ones,
swooshing forever down, down
without the struggle of going up.

so engrossed were they,
they did not see the child
lying in the killing winds,
in the snows of violent suns,
stricken in seeds
        and in bones.

Neither did anyone hear the child cry;

children don't cry like deer.

 *I* FORGIVE YOU

STEVIE SMITH

I forgive you, Maria,
Things can never be the same,
But I forgive you, Maria,
Though I think you were to blame.
I forgive you, Maria
I can never forget,
But I forgive you, Maria,
Kindly remember that.

WARTY BLIGGENS THE TOAD

DON MARQUIS

i met a toad
the other day by the name
of warty bliggens
he was sitting under
a toadstool
feeling contented
he explained that when the cosmos
was created
that toadstool was especially
planned for his personal
shelter from sun and rain
thought out and prepared
for him

do not tell me
said warty bliggens
that there is not a purpose
in the universe
the thought is blasphemy

a little more
conversation revealed
that warty bliggens
considers himself to be
the center of the said
universe
the earth exists
to grow toadstools for him
to sit under
the sun to give him light

by day and the moon
and wheeling constellations
to make beautiful
the night for the sake of
warty bliggens

to what act of yours
do you impute
this interest on the part
of the creator
of the universe
i asked him
why is it that you
are so greatly favored

ask rather
said warty bliggens
what the universe
has done to deserve me
if i were a
human being i would
not laugh
too complacently
at poor warty bliggens
for similar
absurdities
have only too often
lodged in the crinkles
of the human cerebrum
archy

137

OZYMANDIAS

PERCY BYSSHE SHELLEY

I met a traveller from an antique land
Who said: "Two vast and trunkless legs of stone
Stand in the desert. Near them, on the sand,
Half sunk, a shattered visage lies, whose frown,
And wrinkled lip, and sneer of cold command,
Tell that its sculptor well those passions read
Which yet survive, stamped on these lifeless things,
The hand that mocked them and the heart that fed;
And on the pedestal these words appear:
'My name is Ozymandias, king of kings;
Look on my works, ye Mighty, and despair!'
Nothing beside remains. Round the decay
Of that colossal wreck, boundless and bare
The lone and level sands stretch far away."

MY LAST DUCHESS

ROBERT BROWNING

Ferrara

That's my last Duchess painted on the wall,
Looking as if she were alive. I call
That piece a wonder, now: Frà Pandolf's hands
Worked busily a day, and there she stands.
Will't please you sit and look at her? I said
"Frà Pandolf" by design, for never read
Strangers like you that pictured countenance,
The depth and passion of its earnest glance,
But to myself they turned (since none puts by
The curtain I have drawn for you, but I)
And seemed as they would ask me, if they durst
How such a glance came there; so, not the first
Are you to turn and ask thus. Sir, 't was not
Her husband's presence only, called that spot
Of joy into the Duchess' cheek: perhaps

Frà Pandolf chanced to say, "Her mantle laps
Over my lady's wrist too much," or "Paint
Must never hope to reproduce the faint
Half-flush that dies along her throat:" such stuff
Was courtesy, she thought, and cause enough
For calling up that spot of joy. She had
A heart—how shall I say?—too soon made glad.
Too easily impressed: she liked whate'er
She looked on, and her looks went everywhere.
Sir, 't was all one! My favor at her breast,
The dropping of the daylight in the West,
The bough of cherries some officious fool
Broke in the orchard for her, the white mule
She rode with round the terrace—all and each
Would draw from her alike the approving speech,
Or blush, at least. She thanked men—good! but thanked
Somehow—I know not how—as if she ranked
My gift of a nine-hundred-years-old name
With anybody's gift. Who'd stoop to blame
This sort of trifling? Even had you skill
In speech—(which I have not)—to make your will
Quite clear to such an one, and say, "Just this
Or that in you disgusts me; here you miss,
Or there exceed the mark"—and if she let
Herself be lessoned so, nor plainly set
Her wits to yours, forsooth, and made excuse,
Even then would be some stooping; and I choose
Never to stoop. Oh sir, she smiled, no doubt,
Whenever I passed her; but who passed without
Much the same smile? This grew; I gave commands;
Then all smiles stopped together. There she stands
As if alive. Will't please you rise? We'll meet
The company below, then. I repeat,
The Count your master's known munificence
Is ample warrant that no just pretence
Of mine for dowry will be disallowed;
Though his fair daughter's self, as I avowed
At starting, is my object. Nay, we'll go
Together down, sir. Notice Neptune, though,
Taming a sea-horse, thought a rarity,
Which Claus of Innsbruck cast in bronze for me!

139

8 STILL SEPARATE IDENTITIES

THE POEMS

*P*AGES FROM JENNY'S DIARY

LIBBY SCHEIER

1.
Being in the crib
too young to feel like a girl or boy
I remember only one thing:
the green wolf under the bed
sometimes as tiny as a thumb
sometimes as big as a dog
only scary when it was shrinking
or expanding
and me too frightened to even make a noise.

2.
My best photo is me and Bobby
both in cowboy pants and vest
holsters and guns and great big hats
and me almost a head taller than
my boyfriend, and the grown-ups
always saying something about that,
but we don't care.
It's great to be four years old and a cowboy.

3.
I hate skirts, short round things
like lamps that make your legs and bum
cold, and make you feel like a lamp
that at any minute might be put on
someone's table for looking at and
turning off and on.
Besides, me and Bobby like it best
when we're dressed the same.

4.
Being seven was a hundred years older than being
    four. When
I turned seven I was ready to try and meet the
    expectations
of the outside world rather than listen to my heart
    and head.
But sometimes I had to listen to my heart and head
    anyway.

Myth

MURIEL RUKEYSER

Long afterward, Oedipus, old and blinded, walked the
roads.   He smelled a familiar smell.   It was
the Sphinx.   Oedipus said, "I want to ask one question.
Why didn't I recognize my mother?"   "You gave the
wrong answer," said the Sphinx.   "But that was what
made everything possible," said Oedipus.   "No," she said.
"When I asked, What walks on four legs in the morning,
two at noon, and three in the evening, you answered,
Man.   You didn't say anything about woman."
"When you say Man," said Oedipus, "you include women
too. Everyone knows that."   She said, "That's what
you think."

144

Ancestral Burden

ALFONSINA STORNI

You told me: My father did not weep;
You told me: My grandfather did not weep;
They have never wept, the men of my race;
They were of steel.

Speaking thus, a tear welled from you
And fell upon my mouth . . . More venom
Have I never drunk from any other glass
As small as that.

Weak woman, poor woman who understands,
Sorrow of centuries I knew in the drinking of it:
Ah, this soul of mine can not support
All of its weight!

*N*O RESPECT

STEVIE SMITH

I have no respect for you
For you would not tell the truth about your grief
But laughed at it
When the first pang was past
And made it a thing of nothing.
You said
That what had been
Had never been
That what was
Was not:
You have a light mind
And a coward's soul.

*E*XCEPT FOR LAURA SECORD

(or Famous Women from Canada's Past)

SYLVIA MAULTASH WARSH

This nation was founded by men,
fought for bled for
divvied up by men who didn't
eat dinner,
change their underwear,
make holes in their socks,
or father children.
We know this is true because
women are not mentioned in
history books, except for
Laura Secord who invented
ice cream with the help
of her cow.
Except for Laura Secord,
women did not come from England
and France, their footfalls
did not stir the forests,
their soup did not boil in
fireplaces, their laundry
never hung from trees,
so their children remember
them only in dreams.

To Lucasta, on Going to the Wars

RICHARD LOVELACE

Tell me not, Sweet, I am unkind,
    That from the nunnery
Of thy chaste breast and quiet mind
    To war and arms I fly.

True, a new mistress now I chase,
    The first foe in the field;
And with a stronger faith embrace
    A sword, a horse, a shield.

Yet this inconstancy is such
    As you too shall adore;
I could not love thee, dear, so much,
    Loved I not honour more.

146

SIREN SONG

MARGARET ATWOOD

This is the one song everyone
would like to learn: the song
that is irresistible:

the song that forces men
to leap overboard in squadrons
even though they see the beached skulls

the song nobody knows
because anyone who had heard it
is dead, and the others can't remember.
Shall I tell you the secret
and if I do, will you get me
out of this bird suit?

I don't enjoy it here
squatting on this island
looking picturesque and mythical
with these two feathery maniacs,
I don't enjoy singing
this trio, fatal and valuable.

I will tell the secret to you,
to you, only to you.
Come closer. This song

is a cry for help: Help me!
Only you, only you can,
you are unique

at last. Alas
it is a boring song
but it works every time.

$\mathcal{S}$T. GEORGE

NANCY SENIOR

My dragon always loved walks
He used to go to the wall
where the golden chain hung
and take it in his mouth
laying his head on my lap
sideways, so the fire wouldn't burn my skirt

He looked so funny that way
with his wings dragging the floor
and his rear end high up
because he couldn't bend his hind legs

With him on the leash, I could go anywhere
No band of robbers dared attack

This morning in the woods
we had stopped for a drink
where a spring gushes out of a cave

when suddenly, a man in armour
riding a white horse
leapt out of the bushes
crying "Have no fear
I will save you"

And before I could say a word
he had stabbed my dragon in the throat
and leaping down from the horse
cut off his head
and held it up for me to see
the poor eyes still surprised
and mine filling with tears
He hadn't even had time to put out his claws
And the man said
"Don't cry, Maiden
You are safe now
But let me give you some good advice

Don't ever walk alone in the woods
for the next time you meet a dragon
there might not be a knight around to save you"

A NIGHT OF THE FULL MOON

BERT ALMON

The young man can't rest his hands anywhere.
The sleepy doctor flaps the dark film
holding it up to the light, and laughs,
saying to the girl with the punk cut,
"He's broken both of them. You'd better
    tell him."
But he's guessed: *"Tous les deux?"* *"Oui,*
tous les deux," she answers, giggling:
"I guess he won't be driving the Cat for a
    long time."
The fight was over her and he broke his hands
on the other guy, and still lost. Somehow
he kept the girl, but her insouciance puzzles him,
and he says *"Tous les deux?"* again, hoping to hear
they're only joking. The doctor is telling her
how these breaks are hard to set, the small bones
don't stay put. He'll instruct the orderly himself.
The girl casually lights the first cigarette
that she'll place in her lover's mouth.

MARKS

LINDA PASTAN

My husband gives me an A
for last night's supper,
an incomplete for my ironing,
a B plus in bed.
My son says I am average,
an average mother, but if
I put my mind to it
I could improve.
My daughter believes
in Pass/Fail and tells me
I pass. Wait 'til they learn
I'm dropping out.

*I*NDIAN SUMMER

DOROTHY PARKER

In youth, it was a way I had
   To do my best to please,
And change, with every passing lad,
   To suit his theories.

But now I know the things I know,
   And do the things I do;
And if you do not like me so,
   To hell, my love, with you!

APRONS

LEONA GOM

are uniforms, we use them
the way soldiers would, identity,
excuses, to keep ourselves clean,
maybe mostly as good cover, camouflage,
to blend us like wallpaper into
our kitchens, when we work,
tools, weapons (sometimes we forget
the difference) fit our hands
like fingers. we are patriots,
will see the last child evacuated
safely to adolescence.
we have the patience of light
stored in stone.

151

some of us wait too long,
will say we feel undressed without
our aprons, soldiers who wear
their uniforms on the streets,
never want to go back to civvies.

but then there are the others,
those of us who take off our aprons
and move among men like ordinary people,
who get jobs, run for office.
we are not innocents, have experience
at the front. we have learned the tricks,
what happens when someone gives us
a recipe with an ingredient missing,
how when the boss hands us leftovers
we can make casseroles, how to
get out stains before they set
into our personalities.

we have taken off our aprons, but
our hands are full of memories.
sometimes they twist on our laps,
it is dangerous to ignore such need.
they will close around
whatever is put into them.
be careful what you give us.

CRANE LADY

ENOS WATTS

There's the softest tinkling of charms
and an elegant flicking forward
of a braceleted wrist;
then a tiny forefinger
(bent slightly
at the first joint)
makes contact with a button
pressing it
half a centimeter down.
A lever describes an arc
some ten degrees
and instantaneously
another forefinger
docile, though Brobdingnagian,
bends slightly
at the first joint and
forty-five tons of steel plate
fall into place.

INTERIM

ROBYN SARAH

You're on a scaffold, I'm
down below, and you want
to talk, yet—as though
talk, on such a slant, meant
anything; you, teetering there
in your high place, without
a rope, and I in a hole
where I can't see your face?
It's a joke, love. Let's wait
till there's at least a hope
of seeing eye to eye—what?
—talk about talking straight.

I'll stay here and make patterns in the gravel.
(Or, call down, and I'll hand you up your level.)

MAN OVERBOARD

BERNICE LEVER

Here am I left alone
in the boat
with your empty space
trying to steer a course
with only one paddle.

Leaning from side to side
dipping my paddle deep
into the foaming water
I circle crazily
splashing uselessly
unable to see where
you disappeared from our vessel.

It finds, the shore   only
when we both paddle together.

WASHING WINDOWS

BARRY SPACKS

For Laura and Herb Jackson

On a ladder, in an old checkered shirt,
he takes the rag she offers from within.
Their hands begin
slowly to circle, polishing,
and for a time, as particles
on a field of force align,
their hands move one to one,
tight, in a dance, and the glass goes bright
between them, hard, a clearing lens.
They pause and smile, at peace,
each in his own condition.

Union

F.R. SCOTT

Come to me
Not as a river willingly downward falls
To be lost in a wide ocean
But come to me
As flood-tide comes to shore-line
Filling empty bays
With a white stillness
Mating earth and sea.

Union
Exact and complete
Of still separate identities.

from The Prophet

KAHLIL GIBRAN

Love one another, but make not a bond
of love;
Let it rather be a moving sea, between
the shores of your souls.
Fill each other's cup, but drink not, from
one cup.
Give one another of your bread, but eat
not, from the same loaf.
Sing and dance together and be joyous,
but let each one of you be alone,
Even as the strings of a lute are alone,
though they quiver with the same music.

Give your hearts, but not into each
other's keeping.
For only the hand of Life, can contain
your hearts.
And stand together, yet not too near
together:
For the pillars of the temple stand apart,
And the oak tree and the cypress, grow
not in each other's shadow.

9 GREENER GRASS

THE POEMS

$\mathcal{T}$HEN AND NOW

OODGEROO (KATH WALKER)

In my dreams I hear my tribe
Laughing as they hunt and swim,
But dreams are shattered by rushing car,
By grinding tram and hissing train,
And I see no more my tribe of old
As I walk alone in the teeming town.

I have seen corroboree
Where that factory belches smoke;
Here where they have memorial park
One time lubras dug for yams;
One time our dark children played
There where the railway yards are now,
And where I remember the didgeridoo
Calling to us to dance and play,
Offices now, neon lights now,
Bank and shop and advertisement now,
Traffic and trade of the busy town.

No more woomera, no more boomerang,
No more playabout, no more the old ways.
Children of nature we were then,
No clocks hurrying crowds to toil.
Now I am civilized and work in the white way,
Now I have dress, now I have shoes:
"Isn't she lucky to have a good job!"
Better when I had only a dillybag.
Better when I had nothing but happiness.

$\mathcal{G}$REEN RIVER

ANDREW WREGGITT

We are walking away from the week,
up Green River road
A moonscape of clearcut hillsides,
rusted jerry-cans, tipped outhouses
Surveyors' ribbon pokes
up through the dirty mat
of twisted slash
We are moving gladly
up into the hills

In the river, the spawning coho
lie sluggish and black,
turn lamely at the surface and sink
among snags, the sad muddy pools

We are climbing out of the future,
the boggy muskeg, up into slick granite,
following the loggers, this thrust
of gravel and mud

In the evening,
a thin veil of mist grows
like gauze over the slash,
fills the contours,
the red shouts of ribbons and spray paint
A swelling grey cloud

Tonight, everything is healed
in its slow rain

LINES COMPOSED UPON
WESTMINSTER BRIDGE

WILLIAM WORDSWORTH

Earth has not anything to show more fair:
Dull would he be of soul who could pass by
A sight so touching in its majesty:
This city now doth, like a garment, wear
The beauty of the morning; silent, bare,
Ships, towers, domes, theatres, and temples lie
Open unto the fields, and to the sky:
All bright and glittering in the smokeless air.
Never did the sun more beautifully steep
In his first splendour, valley, rock, or hill;
Ne'er saw I, never felt, a calm so deep!
The river glideth at his own sweet will:
Dear God! the very houses seem asleep;
And all that mighty heart is lying still!

YELLOW WARBLERS

GLEN SORESTAD

This summer our backyard has been enlivened
by a pair of yellow warblers whose pale
lemon presence is a first here. They dart
like sun flashes from tree branch
to leafy shrub. The jaunty male sings
his one-note territorial *chip-chip* as he
shifts from poplar to silver maple to red alder.
Clearly they had a nest somewhere near
and my limited knowledge of warblers led me
to suspect our five-foot cotoneaster hedge.
Yesterday I received unwanted confirmation.

I had the clippers out to trim the hedge.
Oblivious, I scissored along, shearing and trimming,
seeking to impose order on this green world—
an unconscious hang-over from Edwardian England.
I leaned over the hedge, just past mid-way
to lop back some disorder, rule raggedness even,
deaf to the uptempo warbler cry that should
have alerted me to my impending trespass.
And then disaster fell. Something in my movement
and my callous pruning dislodged the hedge-home
and out dropped a drab puff of fledgeling warbler,
a fluff of frightened down that lay at my feet
and uttered the equivalent of a lost child's wail.
The parents fretted in agitation about me,
the frenzied male berating me non-stop.

I was appalled. Like that Scottish plowman
two and a half centuries before me. Remorse seized
me by the throat at this gross despoiling.
In the instant I wanted to set things right, yet
knowing that such matters are often difficult, whether
in the realms of birds or men, I knew I must try.

I bent to pick the youngster up from the ground,
but the little one was now gripped by panic
and flapped and hopped across the garden, its confusion
of cries an occasion for more alarm, if possible,
from the frantic parents. In ungainly pursuit
I nabbed it in a row of onions, cupped it
in my palm while it chittered its fright
to all the world, and I stood there
like a grade eight bully accused of harassing
the little kindergarten girls. The parents
were telling me and the neighbourhood what they thought.

I took the trembling fledgeling back to the hedge,
deposited it with care back in its sanctuary,
then took my clippers and left the hedge unfinished.
I sat down at the patio table with my chagrin,
feeling somehow as one who has been exposed
in public for some heinous act. I wondered
whether the parents would desert the violated nest,
whether I'd condemned the young one to starvation,
or to the neighbour's ever-prowling black feline.
The parents worried around the hedge as I sat.

But this morning as I sit at the same table
with my notebook and coffee, the male warbler
flies over to perch above me in the poplar tree
and greet me with a thorough scolding. It has
somehow a definite familiar tone, and I accept it
like a roustabout husband because I have the feeling
that I am being forgiven, though the lecture must be
given nonetheless, as a matter of propriety.
The female is busy in and out the hedge
and this backyard world is for the moment
back to where it was before I took the clippers out.
The untrimmed remnant of hedge may be an affront
to those who put stock in such things,
but to hell with them, I say. To hell with them.

GREENER GRASS

FRANK STEELE

I was born in the city
and have always been
too easy to reach by phone.
Traffic goes by all the time
bumper to bumper, days
of chrome and nights
full of headlights
inside me. I used to hate it
but there you are.

My father was raised in the country
and lives there still, although
long since moved to the city.
Nothing gets to him behind
masses of reserve, old ways
up from the fields or once a week
down chert roads to the post office
wearing a hat that he still tips
to people in the dust of maybe
one car coming.

He envies me still from a distance
no phone can reach or car
connect. Even at this late date,
learning to live my life in traffic,
I wish I could tell him what it meant
once to see the sun come up
across his fields.

162

A TOUGH LIFE

ROBERT CURRIE

I figure you've got it easy
Slop the pigs   milk a few cows
Huh   You shoulda seen the ol days
The first barn we had
was just a hole dug in the hill
with a roof slung across it
Hell that first winter
Maw and Paw took the shack
us boys had to sleep in the barn
Good thing we was bushed
from all the work we did
cause holy ol Nellie it was cold
the barn roof snappin overhead like ice
We'd roll in grey woollen blankets
kind of burrow into a bed of hay
sweet smellin hay   I remember
We'd drift to sleep on a steady rhythm
the horses munchin on their feed
Sometimes after a snowstorm
we'd just lay for hours in the hay
tellin jokes makin up yarns
Wasn't no use gettin up
till Paw had dug us out

What dya mean   it sounds like fun?

163

IN THE MOUNTAINS

LI T'AI-PO
(*Trans. Henry H. Hart*)

You ask me,
Why I live here
In the mountains
Green as jade.
I laugh,
And give no answer.
But within my heart
Is peace.
Indeed
I have hidden in my breast
A paradise
Unknown to worldly men.

The petals of the peach
Fall from the bough
And float in silence
Down the stream.

WHEN I HEARD THE LEARN'D ASTRONOMER

WALT WHITMAN

When I heard the learn'd astronomer,
When the proofs, the figures, were ranged in columns before me,
When I was shown the charts and diagrams, to add, divide, and
measure them,
When I sitting heard the astronomer where he lectured with much
applause in the lecture-room,
How soon unaccountable I became tired and sick,
Till rising and gliding out I wander'd off by myself,
In the mystical moist night-air, and from time to time,
Look'd up in perfect silence at the stars.

To One Who Has Been Long in City Pent

JOHN KEATS

To one who has been long in city pent,
   'Tis very sweet to look into the fair
   And open face of heaven,—to breathe a prayer
Full in the smile of the blue firmament.
Who is more happy, when, with heart content,
   Fatigued he sinks into some pleasant lair
   Of wavy grass, and reads a debonair
And gentle tale of love and languishment?
   Returning home at evening, with an ear
Catching the notes of Philomel,—an eye
   Watching the sailing cloudlet's bright career,
He mourns that day so soon has glided by:
   E'en like the passage of an angel's tear
That falls through the clear ether silently.

*T*HE STREETS OF PURPLE CLOTH

KAREN CONNELLY

She has lost her way in the streets
   of purple cloth and copper skin.
Wandering alone in the city,
   she has touched the veins of silk and gold.
The hilltribe men laugh at her sharp nose, her chalk fingers.
The beggars smile from their caves of tin.

The roads fray to paths scattered with green-eyed goats,
     to old houses splintering now
     and dreaming ghosts.
They lead to temple yards warm with rose light
   where voices chant the bronze language of bells and wind.
The stone shoulders of giants curve to sleep.
Dragons with scales of brilliant glass
   close their tired jaws.

166

The paths darken to wagon ruts
   deep with the hoof-prints of oxen.
They swirl down to blue-roped rivers
   banked by flowers and mud.
Women there stand in waist-deep water,
    twisting silver from their hair.

She walks to a clearness and looks back at the city's old face.
The green light of the field trembles around her.
She hears frogs and crickets but listens
   to the song of her blood.
For the first time, she understands
    the words.

TWO CAMPERS IN CLOUD COUNTRY

(Rock Lake, Canada)

SYLVIA PLATH

In this country there is neither measure nor balance
To redress the dominance of rocks and woods,
The passage, say, of these man-shaming clouds.

No gesture of yours or mine could catch their attention,
No word make them carry water or fire the kindling
Like local trolls in the spell of a superior being.

Well, one wearies of the Public Gardens: one wants a vacation
Where trees and clouds and animals pay no notice;
Away from the labelled elms, the tame tea-roses.

It took three days driving north to find a cloud
The polite skies over Boston couldn't possibly accommodate.
Here on the last frontier of the big, brash spirit

The horizons are too far off to be chummy as uncles;
The colours assert themselves with a sort of vengeance.
Each day concludes in a huge splurge of vermilions

And night arrives in one gigantic step.
It is comfortable, for a change, to mean so little.
These rocks offer no purchase to herbage or people:

They are conceiving a dynasty of perfect cold.
In a month we'll wonder what plates and forks are for.
I lean to you, numb as a fossil. Tell me I'm here.

The Pilgrims and Indians might never have happened.
Planets pulse in the lake like bright amoebas;
The pines blot our voices up in their lightest sighs.

Around our tent the old simplicities sough
Sleepily as Lethe, trying to get in.
We'll wake blank-brained as water in the dawn.

 HILLSIDE THAW

ROBERT FROST

To think to know the country and not know
The hillside on the day the sun lets go
Ten million silver lizards out of snow!
As often as I've seen it done before
I can't pretend to tell the way it's done.
It looks as if some magic of the sun
Lifted the rug that bred them on the floor
And the light breaking on them made them run.
But if I thought to stop the wet stampede,
And caught one silver lizard by the tail,
And put my foot on one without avail,
And threw myself wet-elbowed and wet-kneed
In front of twenty others' wriggling speed,—
In the confusion of them all aglitter,
And birds that joined in the excited fun
By doubling and redoubling song and twitter,
I have no doubt I'd end by holding none.

It takes the moon for this. The sun's a wizard
By all I tell; but so's the moon a witch.
From the high west she makes a gentle cast
And suddenly, without a jerk or twitch,
She has her spell on every single lizard.
I fancied when I looked at six o'clock
The swarm still ran and scuttled just as fast.
The moon was waiting for her chill effect.
I looked at nine: the swarm was turned to rock
In every lifelike posture of the swarm,
Transfixed on mountain slopes almost erect.
Across each other and side by side they lay.
The spell that so could hold them as they were
Was wrought through trees without a breath of storm
To make a leaf, if there had been one, stir.
It was the moon's: she held them until day,
One lizard at the end of every ray.
The thought of my attempting such a stay!

THE FREEZING MUSIC

AL PURDY

There is a music no Heifetz or Paganini knew
it never occurred to them to think of it
—at night when man-sounds fade
the lake is trying to decide about itself
whether it is better to be ice or water
and can't make up its mind
it yearns toward both of them
And little two-inch tubular crystals form
phantoms in the water
when the merest hint of wind comes
they *sing*
they sing like nothing here on earth
nothing here on earth resembles this
this mingled weeping and laughter
sighing between the planets

On earth
I have maneuvered myself near them
my face close to the little tubular crystals
kneeling uncomfortably
on this rocky shoreline near Ameliasburgh
temperature 32 degrees Fahrenheit
shining my flashlight on them
trying to observe the exact instant
water becomes ice
intently observing metamorphosis
but unable to escape myself
Running into the house to escape cold
clapping both hands on my breast grandiloquently
"I have heard the music of the spheres"
But yes I have
yes I have

*I*N NOVEMBER

ARCHIBALD LAMPMAN

With loitering step and quiet eye,
Beneath the low November sky,
I wandered in the woods, and found
A clearing, where the broken ground
Was scattered with black stumps and briers,
And the old wreck of forest fires.
It was a bleak and sandy spot,
And, all about, the vacant plot
Was peopled and inhabited
By scores of mulleins long since dead.
A silent and forsaken brood
In that mute opening of the wood,
So shrivelled and so thin they were,
So grey, so haggard, and austere,
Not plants at all they seemed to me,
But rather some spare company
Of hermit folk, who long ago,
Wandering in bodies to and fro,
Had chanced upon this lonely way,
And rested thus, till death one day
Surprised them at their compline prayer,
And left them standing lifeless there.
There was no sound about the wood
Save the wind's secret stir. I stood
Among the mullein-stalks as still
As if myself had grown to be
One of their sombre company,
A body without wish or will.
And as I stood, quite suddenly,
Down from a furrow in the sky
The sun shone out a little space
Across that silent sober place,
Over the sand heaps and brown sod,
The mulleins and dead goldenrod,
And passed beyond the thickets grey,
And lit the fallen leaves that lay,
Level and deep within the wood,
A rustling yellow multitude.

170

And all around me the thin light,
So sere, so melancholy bright,
Fell like the half-reflected gleam
Or shadow of some former dream;
A moment's golden reverie
Poured out on every plant and tree
A semblance of weird joy, or less,
A sort of spectral happiness;
And I, too, standing idly there,
With muffled hands in the chill air,
Felt the warm glow about my feet,
And shuddering betwixt cold and heat,
Drew my thoughts closer, like a cloak,
While something in my blood awoke,
A nameless and unnatural cheer,
A pleasure secret and austere.

'HOW STILL, HOW HAPPY!'

EMILY BRONTË

'How still, how happy!' Those are words
That once would scarce agree together;
I loved the plashing of the surge—
The changing heaven, the breezy weather

More than smooth seas and cloudless skies
And solemn, soothing, softened airs
That in the forest woke no sighs
And from the green spray shook no tears.

'How still, how happy!' Now I feel
Where silence dwells is sweeter far
Than laughing mirth's most joyous swell
However pure its raptures are.

Come sit down on this sunny stone:
'Tis wintery light o'er flowerless moors—
But sit—for we are all alone
And clear expand heaven's breathless shores.

I could think in the withered grass
Spring's budding wreaths we might discern:
The violet's eye might shyly flash
And young leaves shoot among the fern.

It is but thought—full many a night
The snow shall clothe those hills afar
And storms shall add a drearier blight
And winds shall wage a wilder war

Before the lark may herald in
Fresh foliage twined with blossoms fair
And summer days again begin
Their glory-haloed crown to wear.

Yet my heart loves December's smile
As much as July's golden beam;
Then let us sit and watch the while
The blue ice curdling on the stream.

MARIGOLDS

BLISS CARMAN

The marigolds are nodding;
I wonder what they know.
Go, listen very gently;
You may persuade them so.

Go, be their little brother,
As humble as the grass,
And lean upon the hill-wind,
And watch the shadows pass.

Put off the pride of knowledge,
Put by the fear of pain;
You may be counted worthy
To live with them again.

Be Darwin in your patience,
Be Chaucer in your love;
They may relent and tell you
What they are thinking of.

from THE BURNING OF THE LEAVES

LAURENCE BINYON

Now is the time for the burning of the leaves,
They go to the fire; the nostril pricks with smoke
Wandering slowly into a weeping mist.
Brittle and blotched, ragged and rotten sheaves!
A flame seizes the smouldering ruin and bites
On stubborn stalks that crackle as they resist.

The last hollyhock's fallen tower is dust;
All the spices of June are a bitter reek,
All the extravagant riches spent and mean.
All burns! The reddest rose is a ghost;
Sparks whirl up, to expire in the mist: the wild
Fingers of fire are making corruption clean.

Now is the time for stripping the spirit bare,
Time for the burning of days ended and done,
Idle solace of things that have gone before:
Rootless hopes and fruitless desire are there;
Let them go to the fire, with never a look behind.
The world that was ours is a world that is ours no more.

They will come again, the leaf and the flower, to arise
From squalor of rottenness into the old splendour,
And magical scents to a wondering memory bring;
The same glory, to shine upon different eyes.
Earth cares for her own ruins, naught for ours.
Nothing is certain, only the certain spring.

$\mathcal{P}$ERSUASION

WILLIAM LATTA

Even in the dark
the green urges,
contending its uncoil
from the least
promising miniscule tongue
thrust frangible
above inarticulate ground
into disapproving April air,
driven there
by the law
that the land shall be verdant
in good time
shall defeat the sense
of autumn's brown argument
shall disprove
the negative proposition
of winter.

Beneath my feet
the sprouting assertions
shout green
        and tenderly.

$\mathcal{I}$N MOONLIGHT

LORNA CROZIER

Something moves
just beyond the mind's
clumsy fingers.

It has to do with seeds.
The earth's insomnia.
The garden going on
without us

needing no one
to watch it

not even the moon.

10 THE LEGACY

THE POEMS

The story of replacement

35/10/*Sharon Olds* (USA b. 1942)
Me As My Grandmother/*Rosemary Aubert* (Canada b. 1946)
For a Father/*Anthony Cronin* (Unknown)

Advice for the next generation

What Shall He Tell That Son?/*Carl Sandburg* (USA 1878–1967)
To a Sad Daughter/*Michael Ondaatje* (Canada b. 1943)
The Truisms/*Louis MacNiece* (United Kingdom 1907–1963)

Inspirational ancestors

Great-Aunt Rebecca/*Elizabeth Brewster* (Canada b. 1922)
Request to a Year/*Judith Wright* (Australia b. 1915)
The Legacy II/*Leroy V. Quintana* (Unknown b. 1944)
A Moment of Respect/*Edwin Brock* (United Kingdom b. 1927)

I'm the one to do it now

through *l'oeil de boeuf*/*Paulette Dubé* (Canada)
Pastoral/*Robert Hillyer* (USA 1895–1961)
Digging/*Seamus Heaney* (Ireland b. 1939)
Grandmother/*Barbara Sapergia* (Canada b. 1943)

Back to the source

My Grandmother's Love Letters/*Hart Crane* (USA 1899–1932)
Photograph/*Don Coles* (Canada b. 1928)
Heirloom/*A.M. Klein* (Canada 1909–1972)

Existing still in us

The Elder's Drum/*Molly Chisaakay* (Canada)
Innuit/*Al Purdy* (Canada b. 1918)
On Newfoundland/*Tessa McWatt* (Canada)
The Hoop/*Elizabeth Brewster* (Canada b. 1922)

35/10

SHARON OLDS

Brushing out my daughter's dark
silken hair before the mirror
I see the grey gleaming on my head,
the silver-haired servant behind her. Why is it
just as we begin to go
they begin to arrive, the fold in my neck
clarifying as the fine bones of her
hips sharpen? As my skin shows
its dry pitting, she opens like a small
pale flower on the tip of a cactus;
as my last chances to bear a child
are falling through my body, the duds among them,
her full purse of eggs, round and
firm as hard boiled yolks, is about
to snap its clasp. I brush her tangled
fragrant hair at bedtime. It's an old
story—the oldest we have on our planet—
the story of replacement.

E AS MY GRANDMOTHER

ROSEMARY AUBERT

Sometimes
I look up quickly
and see for an instant
her face
in my mirror,
random tightness
turns my mouth
into a facsimile of hers,
eyes caught oddly
in the glass
make me
into her
looking at me.

Now that she's dead,
I understand
that it is right
that I should age
and wrinkle into her.
It brings her back,
it puts me into
the cycle of family.
We look at all time
with just that
one same face.

 OR A FATHER

ANTHONY CRONIN

With the exact length and pace of his father's stride
The son walks,
Echoes and intonations of his father's speech
Are heard when he talks.

Once when the table was tall,
And the chair a wood,
He absorbed his father's smile and carefully copied
The way that he stood.

He grew into exile slowly,
With pride and remorse,
In some ways better than his begetters,
In others worse.

And now having chosen, with strangers,
Half glad of his choice,
He smiles with his father's hesitant smile
And speaks with his voice.

WHAT SHALL HE TELL THAT SON?

CARL SANDBURG

A father sees a son nearing manhood.
What shall he tell that son?
"Life is hard; be steel; be a rock."
And this might stand him for the storms
   and serve him for humdrum and monotony
   and guide him amid sudden betrayals
   and tighten him for slack moments.
"Life is soft loam; be gentle; go easy."
And this too might serve him.
Brutes have been gentled where lashes failed.
The growth of a frail flower in a path up
   has sometimes shattered and split a rock.
A tough will counts. So does desire.
So does a rich soft wanting.
Without rich wanting nothing arrives.
Tell him too much money has killed men
   and left them dead years before burial:
   and quest of lucre beyond a few easy needs
   has twisted good enough men
   sometimes into dry thwarted worms.
Tell him time as a stuff can be wasted.
Tell him to be a fool every so often
   and to have no shame over having been a fool
   yet learning something out of every folly
   hoping to repeat none of the cheap follies
   thus arriving at intimate understanding
   of a world numbering many fools.
Tell him to be alone often and get at himself
   and above all tell himself no lies about himself,
   whatever the white lies and protective fronts
   he may use amongst other people.
Tell him solitude is creative if he is strong
   and the final decisions are made in silent rooms.
Tell him to be different from other people
   if it comes natural and easy being different.

Let him have lazy days seeking his deeper motives.
Let him seek deep for where he is a born natural.
   Then he may understand Shakespeare
   and the Wright brothers, Pasteur, Pavlov,
   Michael Faraday and free imaginations
bringing changes into a world resenting change.
            He will be lonely enough
            to have time for the work
            he knows as his own.

To A SAD DAUGHTER

MICHAEL ONDAATJE

All night long the hockey pictures
gaze down at you
sleeping in your tracksuit.
Belligerent goalies are your ideal.
Threats of being traded
cuts and wounds
—all this pleases you.
O my god! you say at breakfast
reading the sports page over the Alpen
as another player breaks his ankle
or assaults the coach.

When I thought of daughters
I wasn't expecting this
but I like this more.
I like all your faults
even your purple moods
when you retreat from everyone
to sit in bed under a quilt.
And when I say 'like'
I mean of course 'love'
but that embarrasses you.
You who feel superior to black and white movies
(coaxed for hours to see *Casablanca*)
though you were moved
by *Creature from the Black Lagoon*.

One day I'll come swimming
beside your ship or someone will
and if you hear the siren
listen to it. For if you close your ears
only nothing happens. You will never change.

I don't care if you risk
your life to angry goalies
creatures with webbed feet.
You can enter their caves and castles
their glass laboratories. Just
don't be fooled by anyone but yourself.

This is the first lecture I've given you.
You're 'sweet sixteen' you said.
I'd rather be your closest friend
than your father. I'm not good at advice
you know that, but ride
the ceremonies
until they grow dark.

183

Sometimes you are so busy
discovering your friends
I ache with a loss
—but that is greed.
And sometimes I've gone
into *my* purple world
and lost you.

One afternoon I stepped
into your room. You were sitting
at the desk where I now write this.
Forsythia outside the window
and sun spilled over you
like a thick yellow miracle
as if another planet
was coaxing you out of the house
—all those possible worlds!—
and you, meanwhile, busy with mathematics.

I cannot look at forsythia now
without loss, or joy for you.
You step delicately
into the wild world
and your real prize will be
the frantic search.
Want everything. If you break
break going out not in.
How you live your life I don't care
but I'll sell my arms for you,
hold your secrets forever.

If I speak of death
which you fear now, greatly,
it is without answers,
except that each
one we know is
in our blood.
Don't recall graves.
Memory is permanent.
Remember the afternoon's
yellow suburban annunciation.
Your goalie
in his frightening mask
dreams perhaps
of gentleness.

THE TRUISMS

LOUIS MacNEICE

His father gave him a box of truisms
Shaped like a coffin, then his father died;
The truisms remained on the mantelpiece
As wooden as the playbox they had been packed in
Or that other his father skulked inside.

Then he left home, left the truisms behind him
Still on the mantelpiece, met love, met war,
Sordor, disappointment, defeat, betrayal,
Till through disbeliefs he arrived at a house
He could not remember seeing before.

And he walked straight in; it was where he had come from
And something told him the way to behave.
He raised his hand and blessed his home;
The truisms flew and perched on his shoulders
And a tall tree sprouted from his father's grave.

GREAT-AUNT REBECCA

ELIZABETH BREWSTER

I remember my mother's Aunt Rebecca
Who remembered very well Confederation
And what a time of mourning it was.
She remembered the days before the railway,
And how when the first train came through
Everybody got on and visited it,
Scraping off their shoes first
So as not to dirty the carriage.
She remembered the remoteness, the long walks between
    neighbours.
Her own mother had died young, in childbirth,
But she had lived till her eighties,
Had borne eleven children,
Managed to raise nine of them,
In spite of scarlet fever.

She had clothed them with the work of her own fingers,
Wool from her own sheep, spun at home,
Woven at home, sewed at home
Without benefit of machine.
She had fed them with pancakes and salt pork
And cakes sweetened with maple sugar.
She had taught them one by one to memorize
'The chief end of man is to know God,'
And she had also taught them to make porridge
And the right way of lighting a wood fire,
Had told the boys to be kind and courageous
And the girls never to raise their voices
Or argue with their husbands.

I remember her as an old woman,
Rheumatic, with folded hands,
In a rocking chair in a corner of the living room,
Bullied (for her own good) by one of her daughters.
She marveled a little, gently and politely,
At radios, cars, telephones;
But really they were not as present to her
As the world of her prime, the farmhouse
In the midst of woods, the hayfields
Where her husband and the boys swung their scythes
Through the burning afternoon, until she called for supper.

For me also, the visiting child, she made that world more real
Than the present could be. I too
Wished to be a pioneer,
To walk on snowshoes through remote pastures,
To live away from settlements an independent life
With a few loved people only; to be like Aunt Rebecca,
Soft as silk and tough as that thin wire
They use for snaring rabbits.

1960

REQUEST TO A YEAR

JUDITH WRIGHT

If the year is meditating a suitable gift,
I should like it to be the attitude
of my great-great-grandmother,
legendary devotee of the arts,

who, having had eight children
and little opportunity for painting pictures,
sat one day on a high rock
beside a river in Switzerland

and from a difficult distance viewed
her second son, balanced on a small ice-floe,
drift down the current towards a waterfall
that struck rock-bottom eighty feet below,

while her second daughter, impeded,
no doubt, by the petticoats of the day,
stretched out a last-hope alpenstock
(which luckily later caught him on his way).

Nothing, it was evident, could be done;
and with the artist's isolating eye
my great-great-grandmother hastily sketched the scene.
The sketch survives to prove the story by.

Year, if you have no Mother's day present planned;
reach back and bring me the firmness of her hand.

THE LEGACY II

LEROY V. QUINTANA

Grandfather never went to school
spoke only a few words of English,
a quiet man; when he talked
talked about simple things

planting corn or about the weather
sometimes about herding sheep as a child.
One day pointed to the four directions
taught me their names
    El Norte
Poniente   Oriente
    El Sud

He spoke their names as if they were
one of only a handful of things
a man needed to know

Now I look back
only two generations removed
realize I am nothing but a poor fool
who went to college

trying to find my way back
to the center of the world
where grandfather stood
that day.

188

A MOMENT OF RESPECT

EDWIN BROCK

Two things I remember about my grandfather:
his threadbare trousers, and the way he adjusted
his half-hunter watch two minutes everyday.

When I asked him why he needed to know the time so
exactly, he said a business man could lose a fortune
by being two minutes late for an appointment.

When he died he left two meerschaum pipes
and a golden sovereign on a chain. Somebody
threw the meerschaum pipes away, and
there was an argument about the sovereign.

On the day of his burial the church clock chimed
as he was lowered down into the clay, and all
the family advanced their watches by two minutes.

THROUGH L'OEIL-DE-BOEUF

PAULETTE DUBÉ

no one told me Easter arrives so early
the sun is weakly breathing behind the hill
in the tree the birds mutter as they turn in their sleep
clucking and whispering
my *pepere* shakes me from my quilts
and tucks my nightshirt down my pants

my stomach is shaking
not the scared kind
but a bone cold kind
he tells me to run out my gooselumps
as he jerks my boots up hard to tight them

the door opens
our breath hovers in the air
the sun has a blanket pulled over the hill
the low clouds muffle our sounds
while we walk down on frozen ground
to where the creek offers *l'eau de Paques*

a little blue wind swirls the breath
we stoop to the water
"it is icy damned cold" *Pepere* says
but i can't feel it and he has to
pull my little jar out of the water
when my hand lets go by itself

his dry scratchy brown hands
pull and pat my stupid hand til it moves
then he rolls a cigarette and we smoke
our prize in the mason jar beside us
i smile to his squinty eyes

the house is still breathing quietly when we slip
    through the door
Pepere puts our water in a big white bowl
and drops a white *saule* in it
and puts it all on the table
with *Memere*'s name on a paper

he ruffles my quilts around me and leaves
to tell *Memere* of the miracle
i wriggle from my pants
not wanting to ruin his surprise

$\mathcal{P}$ASTORAL

ROBERT HILLYER

The wise old apple tree in spring,
Though split and hollow, makes a crown
Of such fantastic blossoming
We cannot let them cut it down.
It bears no fruit, but honey bees
Prefer it to the other trees.

The orchard man chalks his mark
And says, "This empty shell must go."
We nod and rub it off the bark
As soon as he goes down the row.
Each spring he looks bewildered. "Queer,
I thought I marked this thing last year."

Ten orchard men have come and gone
Since first I saw my grandfather
Slyly erase it. I'm the one
To do it now. As I defer
The showy veteran's removal
My grandson nods his full approval.

Like mine, my fellow ancient's roots
Are deep in the last century
From which our memories send shoots
For all our grandchildren to see
How spring, inviting bloom and rhyme,
Defeats the orchard men of time.

DIGGING

SEAMUS HEANEY

Between my finger and my thumb
The squat pen rests; snug as a gun.
Under my window, a clean rasping sound
When the spade sinks into gravelly ground:
My father, digging. I look down

Till his straining rump among the flowerbeds
Bends low, comes up twenty years away
Stooping in rhythm through potato drills
Where he was digging.

The coarse boot nestled on the lug, the shaft
Against the inside knee was levered firmly.
He rooted out tall tops, buried the bright edge deep
To scatter new potatoes that we picked
Loving their cool hardness in our hands.

By God, the old man could handle a spade.
Just like his old man.

My grandfather cut more turf in a day
Than any other man on Toner's bog.
Once I carried him milk in a bottle
Corked sloppily with paper. He straightened up
To drink it, then fell to right away

Nicking and slicing neatly, heaving sods
Over his shoulder, going down and down
For the good turf. Digging.

The cold smell of the potato mould, the squelch and slap
Of soggy peat, the curt cuts of an edge
Through living roots awaken in my head.
But I've no spade to follow men like them.

Between my finger and my thumb
The squat pen rests.
I'll dig with it.

$\mathcal{G}$RANDMOTHER

BARBARA SAPERGIA

i remember your hands
making placinta in the Old House
in the sunny kitchen, your hands
strong and warm, shape the batter
on an old wood table scrubbed clean

thinner & thinner, your hands
stretch and pull the batter
thin as paper, thin as onion skins
a thousand times i thought
the skin would tear   you laughed &
held it to the light
the light showed through &
the shape of your face

your hands were brown & strong
but soft   my own young hands
seemed rough when i touched yours
your hands never hesitated, wondering
how much? they reached and scooped
handfuls of raisins and brown sugar
never hesitated, wondering
how is this done? will it tear?
am i doing it right?

my hands have other skills
I place them on the typewriter
and make the keys fly
even with my eyes closed.

193

My Grandmother's Love Letters

HART CRANE

There are no stars tonight
But those of memory.
Yet how much room for memory there is
In the loose girdle of soft rain.

There is even room enough
For the letters of my mother's mother,
Elizabeth,
That have been pressed so long
Into a corner of the roof
That they are brown and soft,
And liable to melt as snow.

Over the greatness of such space
Steps must be gentle.
It is all hung by an invisible white hair.
It trembles as birch limbs webbing the air.

And I ask myself:

"Are your fingers long enough to play
Old keys that are but echoes:
Is the silence strong enough
To carry back the music to its source
And back to you again
As though to her?"

Yet I would lead my grandmother by the hand
Through much of what she would not understand;
And so I stumble. And the rain continues on the roof
With such a sound of gently pitying laughter.

◼ ⱭHOTOGRAPH

DON COLES

This photograph shows a man
who is smiling
standing beside a woman whose smile
may in this moment be just coming
or just going
in a path between a cedar tree
on their right
and unidentifiable bushes on their left
in bright sunlight.
She is wearing a wide white hat
and a loose dress,
he a dark suit, white shirt
with stiff collar,
and a tie with a large knot—
costumes which, since it is evidently
a hot day in summer,
indicate the picture is not recent.
I'm moved to know that in fact
this summer is seventy years ago
and the man and woman
so seemingly at ease here
are my 30-year-old unencountered
grandparents (who died
three years after this photograph
was taken, as we, outside
the photograph, know,
but inside it they do not: my mother
is perhaps almost inside the photograph,
perhaps just beyond it,
perhaps lying in the shade
of the cedar to their right,
and will soon be one year old),
and to know that my mother
will grow older with persons
not present in this photograph,
and so will not adequately be told of
these smiles,this afternoon
of sunlight on a path

(how, partly shadowed
under the wide white hat,
her eyes moved to the sounds
around them, the cicada
in the high trees, how
the warmth of the afternoon lay
across his shoulders
on the dark cloth), the hot green smell
of cedar moving in the mind.
It reminds me of Villon and other
unrecovered seasons, but better than that
it focuses for me a minute when
changeless, constant things fused with
two people who smiled just then
to invincibly form
a space in time which (as perhaps
in that minute they felt, and so
entered it with great anxiety, but
also with great love) that summer
would not carelessly release
but would continue to offer so that
it might one day be acknowledged,
as I would acknowledge it now,
so that they are still there,
or here,
and may be encountered now
if I can make the afternoon
absolute enough, the smell of cedar
endless enough and green
in its summer heat, if I can make
their smiles turn towards her,
standing, now, and older,
and facing them
in the path between the bushes and the cedar
in the bright sunlight
smiling

HEIRLOOM

A.M. KLEIN

My father bequeathed me no wide estates;
No keys and ledgers were my heritage;
Only some holy books with *yahrzeit* dates
Writ mournfully upon a blank front page—

Books of the Baal Shem Tov, and of his wonders;
Pamphlets upon the devil and his crew;
Prayers against road demons, witches, thunders;
And sundry other tomes for a good Jew.

Beautiful: though no pictures on them, save
The scorpion crawling on a printed track;
The Virgin floating on a scriptural wave,
Square letters twinkling in the Zodiac.

The snuff left on this page, now brown and old,
The tallow stains of midnight liturgy—
These are my coat of arms, and these unfold
My noble lineage, my proud ancestry!

And my tears, too, have stained this heirloomed ground,
When reading in these treatises some weird
Miracle, I turned a leaf and found
A white hair fallen from my father's beard.

THE ELDER'S DRUM

MOLLY CHISAAKAY

The smoke rises from the sacrificial fire,
the circle is getting bigger, and many share hope,
the elder begins to drum and circles with song,
my love for the people in the circle exuberates,
the many other times I have shared these rituals,
noticing the whiteness, and the age of my grandfather's hair,
he seems frail and yet the song comes with such clarity,
and my spirit rejoices, in the song of my people,
that we all have the dignity to be,
to determine the spirit, to be like the man who sings,
and yet be proud of the heritage,
our grandfathers leave us the path,
the song, the sacred song.

ꟾNNUIT

AL PURDY

An old man carving soapstone
at the co-op in Frobisher Bay
and in his faded eyes
it is possible to see them
shadowy figures
past the Dorset and pre-Dorset Cultures
5,000 years ago
if you look closely
But the race-soul has drawn back
drawn back
from settlements and landing fields
from white men
into secret vaults
and catacombs of marrow
bone rooms
that reveal nothing
The Innuit which is to say
                    THE PEOPLE
as the Greeks called all foreigners
                    barbaroi
something other than themselves
                    un-GREEK
so the Innuit
          The People
these unknowable human beings
who have endured 5,000 years
on the edge of the world
a myth from long ago
that reaches into the past
but touches an old man still living
Looking into his eyes
it is possible to see the first hunters
(if you have your own vision)

after the last ice age
moving eastward from Siberia
without dogs or equipment
toward the new country
pausing on the sea-ice
for a moment of rest
then pushing on thru the white smother
—Flying generations
leap and converge on this face
an old man carving soapstone
with the race-soul of The People
THE PEOPLE
moving somewhere
behind his eyes

Pangnirtung, 1967

ON NEWFOUNDLAND

TESSA McWATT

We're driving in the car, you and I,
again . . .
(it seems we're always driving somewhere)
Now we're in Newfoundland, on the west coast,
near the top,
near the point where Vikings
(no relatives of mine)
first landed and left their trace in the mist
(cold blue stares, ghost-like on the coast,
penetrating along the shore).
At Sally's Cove just after the sun has set
I see ahead of us five large dark forms with
oversized heads, bushy tails, four thin legs.
We approach,
stop,
and horses,
hushed like the time of day, stand
(just stand) in the middle of the road.

We open our windows (it gets a little darker)
and two of them poke their enormous heads in
the car:
heads, eyes
at my shoulder, horse smell, horse drool on my legs.
One wants in the trunk and nudges the whole car
with its face.
You look at me and we stare
for one moment then
burst into a smile,
the smile of times like this—a smile
of a ghost at a ghost-like hour—
(the same smile in the Dominican Republic
when porpoises chased our sailboat).
We sit silently
and listen to heavy horse breathing,
(our own hearts pounding way up in my ears)
and then I begin to think that
time and love
have banded together and become
phantoms on a deserted highway
awaiting travellers like us
and changing hemispheres to mist,
making cultures and creatures
ghosts of other times when
the sun has set on seven smiling beasts
and ancient cries echo off the shore.

THE HOOP

ELIZABETH BREWSTER

To have grown up the youngest child
of middle-aged parents
meant always to be aware of the past,
to touch their childhoods
like inherited china figurines:

Father at three years old
chased by a turkey gobbler
twice his size

Mother, dressed in her Sunday best,
at a Baptist prayer meeting,
or visiting (against her mother's orders)
old Mary Ellen, the witch
who smoked a pipe
and told fortunes in the tea leaves
if you crossed her palm;

even my brothers and sisters,
remembering all those Christmases
before I was born,
the box of soldiers and the glass fire engine,
and Christmas trees with wax candles,
and lantern slides of someone's trip to Palestine.

Oh, it was past, not present,
that was most real to all of them.
And I, even when I liked the Now
(the iridescent lights
in soap bubbles
or the pink tongue of the kitten
rasping like warm sandpaper
against my fingers)
wanted time to move back, not forward.

Cheated, I always felt cheated
that I never saw Mother sitting
on her long sable hair
before it was ever cut,
before it was fanned with white;

or saw Grandfather the day
he came back from prospecting,
tossing gold nuggets
carelessly
on the kitchen table,
pretending he had lots more of them.

And I wanted to go back in time
further and further
to my Great-Grandfather Solomon
who played the fiddle at dances
and his twin brother David
who left and made his fortune
down in the States,
and the two young girls
they married on New Year's Day
back in 1852.
I wanted to see the river
before anybody had cut the trees

and before that the refugees
coming up from New England
and emigrants crossing the ocean—
I wanted to know what their journeys were like
and where the blue plate came from
I still bring out
sometimes for company

and back to Lincolnshire
the fens
and the hilly cathedral city
and long long ago
maybe marauding Vikings
with blue eyes like my father's
or homesick Roman soldiers
camping in Britain

203

and time unreeling and unreeling
to ancient caves and pyramids
the Golden Age or Eden
primeval chaos
exploding lights

like the lights that will explode (maybe)
at the end of time

when Alpha and Omega meet
and time begins again
circular as the child's hoop
my father played with
made for him by his father.

*M*AKE THE POEMS COME ALIVE

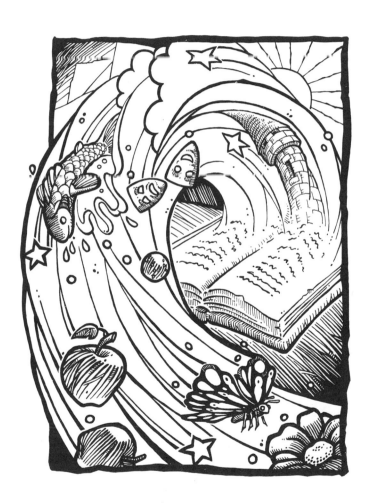

205

1 *T*HE HUNGRY HEART

REFLECTIONS:

> *Life's journey begins with much eagerness and a hunger to discover what the future holds.*

It is our youthful idealism which leads us to explore untravelled worlds with great anticipation. For many, this adventurous spirit lasts a lifetime.

1. In a small group, share descriptions of the most adventurous people you know. What qualities do they have in common? How do they differ from each other?

2. What meanings does the expression "hungry heart" suggest? In what ways do you have a hungry heart?

Standing at the crossroads *(p. 3–4)*
1. Think of the most significant thing that happened to you when you were a child. List specific images you associate with this event.

   Write a poem using these images. Make a comment at the end of the poem about the concept of "crossroads."

2. The speaker in Robert Frost's "The Road Not Taken" (p.3) states that he took the road "less travelled by / And that has made all the difference." Reflect upon a decision that has made all the difference in your life.

   Describe this decision in a personal essay by detailing the alternatives you faced, what the final choice was and the impact it had on your life.

3. The speaker in "Shooting the Sun" by Amy Lowell (p. 4) states that "Four-souled like the wind am I." Identify the various moods this phrase evokes. Find a single picture in a magazine that best captures the effect of this phrase. Add a caption to explain the connection between the illustration and the phrase.

The adventurous spirit *(p. 5–8)*

1. Reflect upon an adventurous moment in your life.

   Write a short anecdote detailing this event, then record it on a cassette. Select an appropriate piece of music to add emphasis and effect to your reading.

2. The speaker in "The Bus" by Leonard Cohen (p. 5) was taken by a fit of fancy to do something extraordinary. People who consistently display such behaviour are sometimes labelled impulsive.

   Relate an interesting story about someone you know, or know of, who is given to what might be considered "strange impulses."

A journey to take *(p. 9–11)*

1. "Girl's-Eye View of Relatives" (p. 9) would seem to suggest that it is necessary for children to eventually leave home even though this may be difficult for some parents to accept.

   Write a letter to your own parents or guardians in which you try to convince them that leaving is something necessary and beneficial for you.

2. Leaving home is often seen as being synonymous with starting a new lifestyle. Imagine yourself as you might be at that time. After you enter your residence, the first thing you do is listen to the recordings on your telephone answering machine. You have had five messages. What are they? Record them on tape to share with the class.

3. The decision to leave home often leaves one with mixed feelings. There can be excitement and anticipation of a new life, but also reluctance to leave behind all that is familiar and "safe." Create a collage of "home" and the "world outside" images that capture these contrasting feelings.

Those who dare *(p. 12–15)*

1. Writers often create characters and situations that symbolically embody values the writers consider important to society. What

values do the characters in this group of poems symbolize? Identify someone you know, or know of, who reflects similar values.

This individual has been nominated to receive the Order of Canada for heroism, and you have been requested to deliver an introductory speech in his/her honour. Write the speech.

2. Review Tennyson's "Ulysses" (p. 12) then choose the role of either Telemachus or Penelope (Ulysses' wife) and write a dramatic monologue as a response to Ulysses' farewell speech. You wish to deliver your parting words to Ulysses personally at the time of his departure. Your speech should reflect your thoughts about his character and his quest.

3. The pursuit of self-fulfilment often seems to involve some degree of self-denial. If you were to devote your life to an ideal at the expense of great personal sacrifice, what would that ideal be?

Thirty years later, you have been asked to write your autobiography to commemorate your achievements. Write the first few pages of the book, beginning with an explanation of why you pursued your dream and why the sacrifice was (or was not) worth it.

The perpetual migration *(p. 16–19)*
1. It might be said that the need to quest is fundamental to the human experience. We explore and take risks as part of the perpetual search for meaning in our lives.

Write a valedictorian speech to your graduating class in which the main theme is the need to quest. Be sure to define what you mean by the term. Incorporate at least one quotation from the poems in this group.

2. A credo is a collection of value statements used to guide one's behaviour. What are the values and ideals reflected by the poems in this chapter?

Drawing upon these values, create a credo that might guide you on your own quest through life.

2 THE CHILD I WAS

REFLECTIONS:

> *As the direction of the road unfolds, much of what is*
> *"childlike" is lost as the emerging adult takes shape.*

Time passes quickly. As childhood disappears so often do simplicity and innocence, to be replaced by the knowledge that we are richer in experience and wisdom.

1. Joni Mitchell once wrote that "Something's lost and something's gained in living every day." Do you think that this is an accurate description of growing up? Explain your opinion.

2. Socrates observed that the more he learned the less he knew. What do you think he meant? What is the wisdom in this?

Where did the children vanish? *(p. 23–25)*

1. Find old photographs which capture the child you used to be. Write captions for each of them. Now, write a poem drawing upon the images and events depicted in the photographs. Finally, pull all these elements together in a display.

2. The speaker in Lisel Mueller's "Palindrome" (p. 23) imagines her double in another universe where time runs backwards. While doing so, she talks about elements of her own past. What elements of your past would you wish to have your double meet? What would best prepare your double for your past?

   Use this list to write your own "Palindrome" poem.

3. As parents watch their children grow they often wonder where time has gone. What memories of your childhood, of the child you used to be, might your parents have?

   Write a journal entry one of your parents might make while reminiscing about you as a child.

The rooms were warm *(p. 25–27)*
1. "Those Winter Sundays" (p. 27) speaks of the everyday, unnoticed things that parents do for us out of love. Make a list of the things your parents do that you ordinarily take for granted.

   Prepare a speech to be given at a party honouring your parents in which you recognize their "austere and lonely offices."

2. Like the speaker in "Childhood" recommends, "close your eyes for a moment, listen." Let your memory drift back as far as it can into your childhood. Select a fond memory associated with your parents and record all the sights, sounds, smells, tastes and touches associated with this memory.

   Use this list to generate your own memory poem.

A little wiser *(p. 28–33)*
1. Reflect upon a childhood memory similar in nature to those in this group of poems. Write a script that would represent the movie version of this experience; record a sound track to accompany your script. Present the finished product to the class as a dramatic reading.

2. Review "Baptism" by Dale Zieroth (p. 32). Assume the role of the speaker in this poem. You and your travelling companion have camped for the night. You feel the need to speak of the traumatic experience that occurred earlier in the day. Write a monologue expressing what you learned about life and your place in it.

Dreams that cannot be *(p. 34–37)*
1. Imagine you are Jenny, from the poem "Reading the Brothers Grimm to Jenny" (p. 37). Twenty years have passed, and you have just discovered this poem in an old scrapbook obviously compiled by your mother.

   Write a letter to your mother in which you talk about certain complexities of life that have made you realize that the world is not "black and white." Be specific, and include such concepts as ambiguity, paradox and compromise.

2. Some people claim it is the pursuit of impossible dreams that makes life worthwhile. They believe that it is not so much whether

we actually attain our dreams that is important, but that we do in fact attempt to fulfil them.

You have been asked to address the youth branch of a political party. Your subject is "The value of dreams-that-cannot-be." Prepare the speech you will deliver.

There used to be a Nord star *(p. 38–40)*

1. Have events ever left you feeling as if you were "floating out to sea?"

   One of the characters in this group of poems has come to you for counselling. You are aware that the first step to solving a problem is understanding and accepting it. Write a dialogue in which you help the character to identify, explain and come to terms with his/her problem.

2. The keynote speaker at the graduation ceremonies in "Graduation Evening" (p. 40) used the metaphor of war for life because the world was at war at that time. What metaphors might be more appropriate to today's world? You might wish to focus on recent positive developments in the world.

   Choose one of these metaphors and develop it into a graduation keynote address that you have been asked to give at your former junior high school's graduation ceremonies.

With age, wisdom *(p. 41–42)*

1. The speaker in "Experience" by Dorothy Livesay (p. 41) makes the point that life's experiences can be both "bitter" and "sweet." Brainstorm a list of specific events or situations that would fit under these two categories in anyone's life.

   Write a retrospective (a review of the past) from the point of view of the speaker in the poem, in which she explains to her grandchildren, aged sixteen and eighteen, why it is necessary to experience both the bitter and sweet for a full life. Use examples from your list to add immediacy to her talk.

2. What wonders might Archibald MacLeish be speaking of in "With Age, Wisdom" (p. 42)? Search through magazines for visual representations of these ideas. Arrange your visuals around a copy of the poem on poster paper.

3 A STRANGER NOW

REFLECTIONS:

> *The journey can become a solitary one; sometimes by choice, sometimes by circumstance.*

Feeling lonely is sometimes unavoidable. At other times we desire solitude and choose to be alone for a variety of reasons.

1. What is the difference between being alone and feeling lonely?

2. An inability to communicate can leave us feeling alone and disconnected. In what ways can the lines of communication between people fail? What is needed to keep the lines open?

What is alone? *(p. 45–47)*
1. Find a picture from a magazine (or any other source) that conveys the sense of loneliness to you. Mount it on paper. Finish the display by writing an explanation of how this photo evokes the feeling of loneliness.

2. Emma LaRocque in her poem "Loneliness" (p. 47) implies that without having experienced loneliness she would not know who she was. How might loneliness help us to understand ourselves better?

   Write a letter to yourself marked "To be opened at a time of loneliness." Explain why it is sometimes necessary to endure loneliness and how it can help you to become a stronger, more fulfilled person.

3. Both "Sanctuary" (p. 46) and "Alone" (p. 47) speak of those times when we seek to be alone. What are the benefits and disadvantages of being alone? Present your thoughts in a personal essay.

Solitude *(p. 48–49)*
1. These poems connect a specific place to the desire to be alone. Describe a place you like to go when you feel the need to be alone. How does this place make you feel?

Combine the descriptions of your special place and of your feelings when you are in it, into a poem. Add a sketch or photograph of this place.

2. Think of the last time you wanted to be alone. What were the circumstances? What benefits did you get from being alone?

Relate the story in a personal essay.

The loneliness we share *(p. 50–53)*
1. It seems musicians often use the theme of loneliness in their songs. Why do you think this is so?

Find a song from your own collection which paints a portrait of a lonely person. Present it to the class or group. Examine the techniques used by the musician to emphasize the impact of the emotion.

2. Assume the role of Billy Joel's piano man (p. 51) playing to a room full of lonely people. What songs will you play for this crowd to get them "feeling all right?" Explain why you chose each song you did.

Broken wires *(p. 54–59)*
1. Compare Tennyson's Ulysses (p. 12) and T.S. Eliot's Prufrock (p. 54) as characters and as symbols of attitudes towards life. With which of these two characters do you most closely identify? How? Why?

Write an introspective of your own personality. Refer to specific details and ideas from the poetry to clarify your comments.

2. "A Note On the Public Transportation System" by Alden Nowlan (p. 59) speaks of a common feeling many of us seem to have when in the company of strangers. What actions do we take to avoid talking to others? Why do we do this?

With at least one other student, dramatize a scene that depicts the idea Alden Nowlan presents in his poem. Create a script that reveals what each character is thinking. Share your script with the class.

Where there's a wall . . . *(p. 60–62)*

1. Every community, however large or small, can sometimes be guilty of building walls around strangers. Reflect upon the situation in your own school or community. How are strangers welcomed into the group? In what ways might it be said that they are made to remain strangers?

   Write a letter of concern to your local community or school newspaper addressing the issue of welcoming newcomers. State your opinion clearly. Support and clarify your position through specific criticisms and suggestions.

2. "40—Love" is a concrete poem. Its physical structure is designed to reinforce its meaning.

   Focusing on the topic of people who are "alone together," create your own concrete poem. Begin by choosing a shape or structure which suggests the idea. Then add words to that structure.

4 *T*HE HUMAN TOUCH

REFLECTIONS:

> At other times, crossroads bring crowded highways and
> close travelling companions.

Love can be expressed in many ways — from showing concern for all humanity to simple affection for another individual. Writers often use the symbol of the hand to express this basic human connection.

1. Identify phrases and advertising images that use the hand to symbolize friendship and caring.

2. What are the many different kinds of love? Do you believe love is important to the individual and to humanity? Why or why not?

Leave me a little love *(p. 65–66)*

1. Extend a human touch to one of the characters from the previous chapter. What could you say or do to make that person feel less isolated?

Write a brief scene depicting your encounter. Include scene directions and dialogue.

2. Make a list of words or phrases which reflect the ways in which we can metaphorically "touch" others. Lightly trace the outline of your hand on a sheet of paper. Fill in this outline with words from your list to create a concrete poem.

No man is an island *(p. 66–70)*
1. Often when something happens to other people, even those we do not know, we are all affected in some way.

Choose a recent or historical event which has somehow affected you. In a personal essay describe the event and explain how and why it had an impact on your life.

2. These selections seem to suggest that we should develop a broader perspective of the world, in which we see each individual as a significant, integral part of humanity.

In a small group create an audio-visual presentation that puts forward this perspective. Create a motto for the project. Share your presentation with the class.

3. Many musicians are becoming more and more involved in promoting a global perspective. Identify some of these artists and the causes they support. Bring some of their songs to be shared with the class.

As a group venture, compose your own song lyrics which advocate involvement in a specific issue, or promote the need for universal empathy and understanding in general. You might wish to use the melody of an existing song.

Helping hand *(p. 71–72)*
1. Many people devote a great deal of their time and energy to helping those in need. Choose someone you know and admire who fits this description.

Write a letter nominating this person for your local humanitarian award. Detail the actions through which he/she demonstrates the quality of caring for others.

2. The school setting affords many opportunities for people to help each other. List the instances when a "helping hand" is possible in some way in your school.

   Write an article for your yearbook, capturing the "caring" quality of your school. Make specific references to people, events, and the reactions of those involved in what happened as well as those who were "witnesses."

3. Reflect upon a time when you went out of your way to help someone, a time when you felt virtue as a "sunrise in the belly."

   Summarise the circumstances involved, and try to recall as accurately as possible both the reaction of the recipient of your deed and your own feelings at the time.

Kindred spirits *(p. 73–74)*

1. Reflect upon stories, movies or television programs you know that contain a memorable friendship. Describe the relationship between the characters in them. What impact does this relationship have on the rest of the story? Present your findings as a magazine article.

2. "First Love" (p. 74) recounts a time when a mother and daughter shared a lighthearted moment because of something unpredictable the daughter had done. What have you done that your parents found astonishing or funny? Recount this humorous incident in a narrative essay.

I knew love when it came *(p. 75–76)*

1. Brainstorm a list of quotations from poems or songs that reflect sentiments on love similar to those in this group of poems. Collect pictures that symbolize the power of love.

   Organize these elements artistically to create a poster which presents your personal definition of love.

2. What is the world around you saying about love? Record what you see and hear on the subject of love during the course of a normal day.

   Write an analysis of your findings, drawing conclusions about society's attitudes towards love.

Marriage is not a house *(p. 76–78)*

1. If marriage is not a house, what is it? Make a list of observations about what marriage is.

   Create a concept map. Place the word marriage in the middle of a piece of poster paper. Arrange your observations regarding marriage around the central concept. Draw lines between these observations showing logical groupings and connections.

5 THE LAST JOURNEY

REFLECTIONS:

> *Farewells are inevitable as we each choose different paths*
> *or reach journey's end.*

Death is a natural part of the life cycle. It defines the end of the journey and serves to remind us that life must not be wasted.

1. In what ways might death be said to give meaning to life?

2. Describe some of the different attitudes we have towards death.

All things must pass *(p. 81–84)*

1. Brainstorm a list of common images that might be used to express an observation on death. Using the method of antithesis that Williams uses in "The Term" (p. 82) as a model, employ one of the images on your list to write a poem.

2. Create a conversation between Hamlet and the coyote of "Bugs Bunny" fame. In their talk, the two characters should explore the effect their differing views of mortality have upon them. Refer to details from their respective settings and stories.

There is a pause *(p. 85–86)*

1. List the images in the poems of this group. What mood do they create?

Make a list of other images which might hold the same impact. Using one or more of these images, write a poem which attempts to create a similar mood. You might wish to emulate the style of "The mists at Asuka" (p. 86).

Life goes on *(p. 87–91)*

1. Housman in "Is my team ploughing" (p. 88) seems to suggest that the life of an ordinary individual does not have a lasting impact on other people; many people would disagree. What do you think?

   Write a letter to A.E. Housman. Comment upon his philosophy and express your own ideas on this matter.

2. The speaker in Joan Finnigan's "My Seven Deaths" (p. 89) recalls her "encounters" with death. Answer the question that the poet raises at the end of the poem. What "deaths" have you survived and what have they taught you about life?

I am not resigned *(p. 92–95)*

1. Each of the speakers in this group seems to reveal a reluctance or a refusal to accept the reality of death. Do their views reflect a positive attitude towards life, or a negative attitude towards death?

   Create a dialogue between two of the speakers in which they explain their differing reasons for not being resigned to death.

Part of the natural cycle *(p. 95–96)*

1. Death is part of a natural cycle, and can often be seen as a beginning or continuation rather than an ending.

   Search through magazines for pictures that might symbolize death, rebirth and life. Arrange these images in a graphic essay that communicates the ideas presented in the poems of this group.

2. Create a visual presentation that parallels the life cycle of a human and that of another natural entity such as a tree. Write a brief description of the various stages in each life cycle, outlining how human life might be seen in terms of its parallel in nature.

We need not dread *(p. 97–98)*

1. Imagine that your much younger brother or sister has experienced the death of a favourite pet. This has left him/her frightened and in need of an explanation.

   Write a dialogue in which you try to explain death and also allay any fears he/she has.

6 $\mathcal{B}$ROKEN IMAGES

REFLECTIONS:

> *Some of our reflections might raise doubts about the nature of the journey, creating the impression that we are travelling in the dark.*

We live in a world of paradoxes and complexities that challenge our philosophies and belief systems. While such experiences can leave us frustrated and frightened, it is with an open mind that we will learn from life's mysteries.

1. The philosopher Socrates (c470-399 BC), stated that the more he learned, the less he knew. Discuss this paradox.

2. Identify contemporary and historical examples of how doubting and/or inquisitive minds have led to change and positive reform in many areas of life.

Fear and doubt *(p. 101–102)*

1. Describe a time when you felt uncertain about the direction your life was taking. Did you feel a little "lost" as the speaker in Margaret Atwood's "Provisions" (p. 102) seems to do, or were you reasonably comfortable with your uncertainty as the speaker in Graves' "In Broken Images" (p. 101) would appear to be?

   Describe the circumstances or event that led to your feeling this way. Explain your thoughts at the time.

2. We have all met people who believe that their opinions on any subject cannot possibly be wrong — they are confident to a fault. What do you think motivates people to act this way? What effect might such an attitude have on other people?

Assume that you have a friend who frequently behaves in just this way. How would you (tactfully) tell your friend that such an attitude might well alienate other people? In your explanation, suggest how doubt might be considered a strength rather than a weakness.

Fearful symmetry (*p. 103–104*)
1. The rhythm of William Blake's "The Tyger" (p. 103) is similar to the rhythm of "Twinkle twinkle little star." What effect does this create?

Using the same rhythm, write a poem about a subject that you find particularly paradoxical.

Fate intervenes (*p. 105–109*)
1. There are times when events seem to happen no matter what we do. Sometimes these are negative; many times they are positive. Write a narrative essay describing a time in your life when a specially positive event (that was completely unexpected) took place.

2. How did you get to where you are now? In the same manner as John Hartford's "I Would Not Be Here" (p. 105) trace the steps by which you came to be in this English class. You might wish to take the long view tracing the steps over the years or you might wish to shorten the timeframe. Try to convey the same sense of cause and effect relationships found in the poem.

Through purblind night (*p. 110–112*)
1. Select several phrases and images from the poems in this group that seem to you particularly effective. Identify the mood each evokes.

Create a visual rendition of one or more of these poems in a collage of magazine pictures or your own original artwork. Try to convey a mood similar to that found in the poems.

2. Identify the extended metaphors in each of the poems of this group and interpret the way in which they develop the themes of

the poems. Make a list of other suitable metaphors that might convey a similar theme.

Choose one of these metaphors and develop it into a poem.

Nothing to do but wait *(p. 112–115)*
1. What ideas are central to the poems in this section? As a group, discuss the most effective way to dramatize these ideas using all of the members of the group. You might wish to use props in your presentation.

2. Prepare a dramatic reading of one of these poems. Record it on either audio or video tape and include music and sound effects. Share your recording with the class.

Even in the darkest hour *(p. 116–117)*
1. You have been invited to write the preface for a book, entitled "In The Face of Adversity," which deals with the theme of overcoming hardship. You have decided to use one or more of the poems in this group to provide ideas and quotations for the preface.

7 $\mathcal{P}$LAYING THE FOOL

REFLECTIONS:

> *Questions concerning the nature and integrity of people*
> *might also arise provoking criticism and a call for change.*

The character who plays the fool is a versatile tool in satire for revealing human shortcomings such as greed, prejudice, and hypocrisy.

1. Search through issues of your local newspaper for satirical cartoons and analyze them for tone and object of attack. Do you agree with the satirist? Why or why not?

2. Make a list of common failings in human nature that you think should be improved upon. Make another list of the "good points" of human nature. Debate whether human nature is predominantly positive or negative.

Fools rush in *(p. 121–122)*

1. Reflect upon a humorous incident when you, or someone you know, did something foolish or mildly embarrassing.

   Write a humorous anecdote that relates the details of this incident and concludes with a moral about human behaviour.

2. As a group, satirize a common and relatively innocent human folly that reveals a lack of common sense. Present your satire as a humorous dramatization. Keep in mind that the purpose of satire is to promote change, not to hurt feelings.

Consistent with peopuls beleef *(p. 122–125)*

1. Review "Mending Wall" by Robert Frost (p. 124) and, using the details provided in the poem, list the character traits of both neighbours. Then compile a list of possible arguments each individual might use in trying to persuade the other to the opposite way of thinking.

   Present this information in the form of a dialogue in which the two characters debate why they should or should not keep the wall that separates their properties. Attempt to capture the personality of each neighbour in your presentation.

The untutored fool *(p. 126–127)*

1. Create the dialogue that occurs when a "shallow" individual encounters an overly sophisticated, worldly type in a Museum of Modern art. The two happen to meet in front of a painting by Picasso — what conversation takes place between them?

2. Archy, from Don Marquis's "The Hen and the Oriole" (p. 126) seems to suggest that physical beauty is revered in our culture. Do you agree or disagree with this viewpoint? Brainstorm examples to support your opinion.

   The Human Rights Commission has asked you to present a report giving your views on the issue of discrimination based upon physical beauty. Write the report in which you support your views with specific examples.

More knave than fool *(p. 128–131)*

1. Discuss the meaning of integrity. List examples of people who display this quality.

Your younger brother or sister has recently been caught cheating or stealing, and you wish to talk to him/her about what integrity means and why you think it is an important quality. Write the words of advice you will offer.

2. Consider the student's actions in "Substitute" by Shirley Paustian (p. 128) and decide what they might suggest about his character. If you were the teacher in this situation, how would you approach the student at the end of the class? What would you like to say to this individual? Explain your rationale in writing.

A mask of virtue *(p. 132–136)*

1. How would you define hypocrisy? Explain the hypocrisy in each of the poems in this group.

   Write a letter to one of the characters in the poems, explaining how you think he/she is being hypocritical. To establish a tone of friendly concern, show that you understand why the character reacted in this way.

2. Make some gentle fun of yourself by creating a list of "commandments" that every one *but* you should have to follow. Develop this list into a poem where you condemn yourself with your own words.

The egocentric *(p. 137–140)*

1. Consider "My Last Duchess" by Robert Browning (p. 138). Analyze the character of the Duke. Now assume the role of the Count's emissary to whom the Duke has been speaking. You were sent to speak to the Duke on behalf of the Count and to form an opinion on the man's character.

   Drawing upon the details of your analysis, write a report to the Count in which you present your impressions of the Duke. Conclude by offering your recommendations regarding the proposed marriage between the Duke and the Count's daughter.

2. Review "Ozymandias" by Percy Bysshe Shelley (p. 138). What would you say to a future leader who was exhibiting signs of becoming another Ozymandias?

   Write a letter to this hypothetical leader in which you warn him/her of the futility of such "passions." Cite images and quotations from the poem.

8 $\mathcal{S}$TILL SEPARATE IDENTITIES

REFLECTIONS:

> *New avenues will be forged in the evolution of relation-*
> *ships between women and men.*

Society's expectations of each gender's role have been changing in recent years as we move towards a more equitable relationship between the sexes. With greater empathy and respect, we can achieve a union of still separate identities.

1. To what degree has there been significant change in the role expectations of men and women in society today? To what extent are you, your family and friends involved in non-traditional roles?

2. What particular role expectations do we have of each gender? Which of these do you think ought to be changed? Which should remain the same? Why?

Ancestral burden *(p. 143–145)*

1. The speaker in "Pages from Jenny's Diary" by Libby Scheier (p. 143) refers to "expectations of the outside world." What do you think she means?

   Assume that Bobby found Jenny's poem years later and wrote a letter to tell her he empathized with her feelings. He also felt expectations from the outside world as a result of his gender. Draft the letter he might have written and include specific examples.

2. "Myth" by Muriel Rukeyser (p. 144) seems to suggest that there is a male bias in our language which contributes to male/female inequality. Do you agree? List examples of words and expressions that support your opinion.

   Work in a small group and debate whether the English language should be changed to eliminate words and expressions that might be seen as containing a male bias. Have one half of the group take the positive side and the other half take the negative. Be sure to identify the advantages and disadvantages of both positions.

Have no fear, I will save you *(p. 146–149)*
1. Create a character that corresponds to the stereotyped image of either the "macho" male or the "sweet young thing" female. Your creation is to be interviewed on a radio broadcast. Draw up a list of questions that will help the announcer uncover the character's true personality, and why he/she feels his/her ideals are essential, even in modern society. With the help of a partner, record the con versation on a tape to "broadcast" to the rest of the class.

2. Much is made today of changing role expectations of men and women. But how much have things really changed?

   Conduct a survey to determine the five most popular male and female television and/or movie stars. Make sure your survey includes both male and female respondents. Present your findings in a report. Do you think the results indicate a change in attitudes? Why or why not?

We have taken off our aprons *(p. 149–152)*
1. Identify a female you respect who reflects the sentiments of one of the characters in this group of poems.

   Write this individual a letter, enclosing a copy of the poem that reminds you of her. Explain what positive links you make between her and the character in the selection you have chosen.

2. List the traditionally male-dominated occupations into which women are currently making successful inroads. List the traditionally female roles that men are currently taking on.

   Write a feature report for a Canadian news magazine exploring the degree to which traditional gender role boundaries are being broken.

3. Examine the advertisements in a popular general interest magazine. Record the ways in which males and females are portrayed. On the basis of this information arrive at some conclusions regarding the degree to which current role changes replace traditional

stereotypes. Write a brief report commenting on current attitudes towards gender roles in our society.

Union of still separate identities *(p. 152–154)*

1. Discuss the meaning of the title of this group of poems. How, giving specific examples of behaviour and/or attitudes, would you interpret "a union of still separate identities?" Depict this concept visually with a collage or poster.

2. The poems in this group make effective use of metaphors and images that convey a sense of "union of still separate identities." Create another metaphor that conveys a similar effect. Develop this into a poem.

9 GREENER GRASS

REFLECTIONS:

> *If life at times seems too complex and overwhelming, refuge can be sought in the simplicity and peace of a greener, more natural world.*

Nature has long been seen as a place where we can escape the complexities of life and restore our health and happiness.

1. Do you think nature is an integral part of our lives? Explain.

2. Do you feel more "at home" in the city or in the countryside? Share your explanation with the members of your group.

3. In what ways do some people show a disregard for nature? How do some other people demonstrate an affinity with the natural world?

To impose order on this green world *(p. 157–161)*

1. Identify examples of how Western civilization might be said to have imposed order on nature. Does this enforced order conflict with nature's own plan, or does it enhance it?

Express your opinion in a collage or poster, using your own artwork, sources from magazines and newspapers, or both.

2. Think of a natural setting you know or have heard about that has been transformed by urbanization. Create a list of words and phrases that describe the setting before and after the development. Using these images, write a poem that develops the idea that cities have been encroaching upon nature.

3. Global concern for the environment is growing as we become increasingly aware of the consequences of our actions. Organizations concerned with this issue are becoming more political and are using advertising as a means of promoting awareness.

   Design an advertisement to encourage people to become aware and responsible in their actions towards the natural world.

4. What would you say to a class of elementary students to make them more aware of humanity's need to look after the environment?

   Create a puppet show that communicates your ideas. Write the script, make the puppets, rehearse your play, and present it to your own class. If possible, arrange to take your show to a local elementary school classroom.

227

The grass is greener (p. 162–164)
1. What mood does the second stanza of "In the Mountains" (p. 164) create?

   Describe in four short lines the strongest emotional response to nature you have ever experienced. Use calligraphy or graphics to create a display of your work.

2. Write a dialogue between two friends, one of whom lives in the city and the other in the country. Have each individual try to convince the other to move to their respective surroundings. Focus on the benefits that might be gained by such a move.

Long in city pent (p. 164–167)
1. For all of the people in these poems, nature seems to offer a form of escape from the city. When you feel a need to escape, in which particular natural setting would you choose to be?

With as much detail as possible, describe what it is about this setting that affects you.

2. Would you like to make your life more simple? How would you do it?

   Imagine that a friend has become caught up in the daily affairs of life and is working too hard. You know he/she is unhappy but cannot seem to "get off the treadmill". You are concerned for your friend's well-being and decide to offer some advice. Write a letter in which you outline some concrete suggestions.

Some magic of the sun *(p. 168–173)*
1. Robert Frost uses an extended metaphor in "A Hillside Thaw" (p. 168) to help the reader visualize the natural phenomena he observed.

   Choose a common natural phenomenon and describe it with the use of an extended visual metaphor. Like Frost, do not state explicitly in your poem what natural event you are describing.

2. Al Purdy, in his poem "The Freezing Music" (p. 169) seems to suggest that nature is filled with musical sounds that we might hear if we listen closely enough. Write a poem that tries to recreate some of nature's music.

The certain spring *(p. 174–175)*
1. The poems in this group seem to suggest that the cycles of Nature would continue even without us. Review the poems and make a list of ways they imply that this sentiment is true. Add to the list by citing events from your own experience that support this way of thinking.

   If the Earth were given a human voice what would it say to us?

2. Take a walk on a spring day.(You might have to do this in your imagination.) Make a note of all the things you see that confirm the sentiments of renewal expressed in these poems. Write a "Rites of Spring" article or poem.

10 THE LEGACY

REFLECTIONS:

> *As the journey draws to a close, our reflections of life*
> *become a legacy for the next generation of travellers.*

As each generation is succeeded by another, we gain an appreciation of the connectedness between people of different eras. The legacy of humanity reaches back into the past and forward to the future.

1. What is there to be gained from previous generations? What specifically is handed on from one generation to the next?

2. Some people believe that genetic make-up determines who we will be. Others believe that life's experiences have more influence on our character. In a small group, debate both these points of view.

The story of replacement *(p. 179–180)*
1. Collect some old photographs of your family. List their influences on your identity. Create a visual presentation of your heritage by combining these photos with a photo of yourself. Add a brief essay outlining your relatives' legacy to you.

2. The poems in this group seem to stress the genetic heritage that is passed on to each successive generation — the "story of replacement." There are other qualities that are passed on by the older generation. What values and behaviours have you picked up from the significant adults in your life?

   Write a letter to an adult who has had an important influence upon the formation of your character. Acknowledge his/her impact on your life.

Advice for the next generation *(p. 181–185)*
1. What advice — based on your own experiences so far — will you give your children?

Arrange this information artistically on a blank sheet of paper. Mount it on a slightly larger sheet of poster paper. Title your display.

2. Reflect upon advice you once received from an older person that, at the time, fell upon deaf ears but has since come to make sense.

Write to that person reminding him/her of the advice he/she tried to give to you. Recall your reaction at the time and explain what has happened since to make you realize the advice offered was good.

Inspirational ancestors (p. 185–189)

1. People receiving awards often pay tribute to those who were an inspiration to them. Identify (or invent) an inspirational ancestor of your own and record details of this individual's actions and influence on your life so far.

Write an award acceptance speech in which you explain the effect this person has had on you. Include an anecdote or a description of this individual's greatness.

2. Imagine how rewarding it would be to discover that you have had an inspirational effect on someone of the next generation.

In what way would you like to be an inspiration? Write a tribute to yourself from the point of view of someone you have inspired. What would you like to hear someone say about you?

I'm the one to do it now (p. 189–193)

1. Write a letter to the person who will be your great-great-grandchild. Tell him/her about yourself and your immediate family. Identify family characteristics, and outline the traditions you hope they will continue to observe. Explain why this is important to you.

2. The speakers in "Digging" (p. 192) and "Grandmother" (p. 193) each admire a relative for a particular skill. They recall how adept that relative was and try to relate their own skills in comparison.

Using vivid images, describe a skill that you admire in one of your relatives. In your writing, be sure to capture a vivid description of your relative performing this skill.

Back to the source *(p. 194–197)*

1. Old family photographs can be fascinating, particularly when you consider the context in which the pictured moment occurred.

   Find an old family picture with a hidden story, the details of which you know or can research. Mount the picture and below it supply particulars of the story and the people who could be standing just outside of the photograph. (If you can't find a family photograph any one will do.)

Existing still in us *(p. 198–204)*

1. Like the Vikings of Tessa McWatt's "On Newfoundland" (p. 200) we are currently leaving our "trace in the mist." History has a tendency to blur the reality of the people who lived in the past. What aspects of our society would you preserve in order to present an accurate picture to a generation two thousand years from now?

   Collect material for a time capsule. Base your selections on those things that would best capture our legacy for the future.

2. In "The Hoop" (p. 202) Elizabeth Brewster confesses a desire to discover the legacy of her ancestry. What things from your past would you like to discover more about?

   Capture your personal heritage by mentioning the things you would like to see on a trip backwards through time. Use a poetic structure similar to "The Hoop." How far back would you like to travel?

3. What material heirlooms would you like to leave for your future relatives? Write a note for each of the objects you choose explaining its significance to you, your family, and the future. Present this as an annotated inventory of your personal legacy.

$\mathcal{T}$HE *REFLECTIONS* JOURNAL:
AN INDEPENDENT PROJECT

PURPOSE:

This journal assignment has been designed to provide a framework within which you can approach the study of poetry independently. It is also a place to reflect upon your own experiences and to connect them to the poetry you read.

FORMAT:

The *Reflections* Journal is actually a mixture of journal and scrapbook. You will be free to use many different modes of communication: personal and analytical writing, songs, photos, mini collages, stories, your own poetry or artwork, anything which effectively communicates your message.

There are two components to each Journal entry:

1. *Reflections:*

   After reading the poem, record your thoughts and reactions. How does the poem work? What comments can be made about poetic technique? What observation about life do you think the poet is trying to make? How does the poem make you feel? Why?

   This writing explores the poem. It should be organized in paragraphs.

2. *Connections:*

   This is the scrapbook component where you connect the poem to the world around you. Suggestions here are limited only by your imagination.

   Clip related pictures, advertisements, and/or articles from newspapers and magazines. Refer to the movies and television shows you watch. Write your own poetry. Create artwork inspired by the poetry. Include your own photographs. Write stories. Add songs.

Make as many connections as possible between the poems
you select and the world in which you live. Include a written
explanation of these connections.

PROCEDURE:

1. Read as much of the poetry in this anthology as you have time for.
    At this stage you are reading to discover which poems you wish to
    select for further reflection.

2. Note the structure of the anthology. Each of the chapters focuses
    on a theme which is divided into several sub-themes or ideas.

3. Select an organizational approach. We recommend you use the
    structure of this anthology. You might choose to explore one poem
    from each chapter or, alternatively, you might choose one chapter
    and explore all the groups within it.

4. Choose the poems. Complete the *Reflections* and *Connections* com-
    ponents of the journal.

READING POETRY

LARRY LIFFITON & JOHN McALLISTER

"I, too, dislike it . . ." So begins the first poem in this anthology. Many people claim to dislike poetry, yet it has endured longer than almost any other form of writing. Why? Poetry conveys our strongest emotions and our most significant experiences through language that is both immediate and real. As Marianne Moore suggests in "Poetry," it provides "a place for the genuine." Poetry is a powerful reflection of the world around us.

Poems are mirrors. They reflect vivid images of who we are and the world that is ours. However, while the images themselves may be clear enough, their real significance is often merely suggested. To fully understand the effect the poet is trying to create the reader must reflect upon the experiences of his/her own life. In doing so it becomes possible to piece together a personal version of how the poem works and how it relates to the reader's own experience. This interpretation can then be compared to the interpretations of others in order to arrive at further understandings.

Meaning is not the only sense to be made of a poem. We must also learn to appreciate its performance. Archibald MacLeish says that "A poem should not mean/ But be." After all, a poem is itself an experience. It must be entered into, lived, and made our own.

In order to do this, a poem must be read and reread frequently. Like music, the more we listen to it the more we understand and appreciate the subtle nuances of that experience. A poem should also be read out loud so that the ear can catch the sound of the performance. Poets often choose words for their musical effect as much as the meaning they might carry.

There is no formula to understanding poetry. You must simply get involved with it. Talk about poetry. Try writing some poetry. Above all else, find some poems you really like and live with them for a while, for poetry requires its own reflection. Give the poems time to speak to your experience. Listen to the way they speak and discover what they say about being alive in this world.

$\mathcal{S}$EXISM IN LITERATURE— ONE VIEW

PAT KOVER

> *No man is an island entire of itself; every man is a piece of*
> *the continent, a part of the main*
>
> (John Donne 1571?-1631)

For many years I accepted without question that the literary giants who loomed so large in my education held "the mirror up to nature," that they reflected reality. It did not occur to me that their view of the world had been shaped by their own experience and personality, and by the beliefs and customs of the time and place in which they lived. And that, as others had shaped their understanding of the world, so they in turn helped to shape mine. Through their words I learned what was valued, what was despised, who deserved to be praised, and who merited being metaphorically ground into the dust.

As we stand on the threshold of a new millennium, gifted with hindsight and the new awareness of our times, it seems obvious that the ideal offered was always male. It was "man" who overcame all adversities; who was brave; and who valued the "higher" functions of will and reason. Although he protected the weak, he despised any evidence of weakness in himself. Most importantly, he put public considerations before personal, and was able to subdue his emotions in order to cling to his lofty goals.

It is almost four hundred years now since John Donne wrote that "No *man* is an island. . . ." Should I, the product of apparently more enlightened times, take immediate exception to his using the word "man?" Should I berate him for an implied denigration of woman? Should I object when Sir Richard Lovelace (1618-1658) explains "To Lucasta, Going to the Wars:" *I could not love thee dear, so much/ Loved I not honour more?*

I would suggest that to do so would be a much greater offence against the human spirit than any I might consider Donne or Lovelace or any other writer to have committed in the past. They wrote, as I do, in the context of their own times, using the common idiom of their culture. I too write in the particular context of my times and my culture — a framework probably as alien to 17th century "man" as theirs is to me. The future may find my view as limited and limiting as I find theirs.

Indeed, mingled with my love for such poets as Donne and Lovelace is discomfort, for I am never quite sure whether they intend me, as a woman, to be part of their audience. And yet with all my heart I rejoice that I know them, for it is in being exposed to a wide variety of literature from many centuries and many cultures that we become aware that there are numerous ways of understanding what it means to be human. Thus influenced and provoked to think deeply by myriad minds, we become more human. If we refuse to read the work of those whose viewpoints might seem on the surface narrow and unacceptable, are we not then guilty of the same intolerance of which we accuse them?

Let us not fall into the trap of viewing humanity through the lens of an unquestioning orthodoxy. What frees me to be the person I am is precisely the recognition that there is no single superior human nature. And what allows me to reach this understanding is largely that I have been exposed to many points of view. The best means of recognizing the limitations of the world view of others, including the great writers of the past, their sexism, racism and ethnocentrism, is to read them — along with many others. To insulate ourselves from them is only to give them greater power.

Like Tennyson's great hero Ulysses, I am a part of all that I have met. Our literature is the story of our past, of the evolution of human relationships; the attitudes these writers present are embedded in our culture. Nor should we forget that the writer's is only one voice in the conversation. The other voice, that of the reader, alters not only with the changing of generations but also with the evolving contexts within one lifetime, and so creates new understandings, new meanings. Though new understandings may render some of their views unacceptable, there yet remains something universal which speaks to all people and all times, for great writers not only reflect their time but transcend it.

Almost two thousand years ago the Roman playwright Terence wrote: "I am a person, and nothing human can be alien to me." *Homo sapiens* we have dubbed ourselves: "the knowing ones." For many generations, writers assumed a knowledge of human nature. And yet our most important characteristic is surely not that we know, but that we learn. We learn from our experience, and from our interaction with others and the world around us. Exposed to many ways of being human, we learn that indeed, nothing human can be alien to us. The more information we have, the more effective is our learning.

The writers of the past believed they espoused the loftiest principles. They had as their goal the good of humanity; they believed they were right. Their mistake was to believe that all others were wrong. We seem at long last on the verge of recognizing that our common humanity lies not in lofty ideals to which few can aspire, but in the experiences we all share. Let us not repeat the mistakes of the past by silencing those whom we believe to be "wrong." It is when we come together, past, present and future, African, Asian, American and European, men and women, that we can celebrate all that we can offer each other through our uniqueness.

Union
Exact and complete
Of still separate identities.

Every effort has been made to trace the ownership of all copyright material and to secure the necessary permissions to reprint the selections. In the event of any question arising as to the use of any of the material, the editor and the publisher, while expressing regret for any inadvertent error, will be happy to make the necessary correction in future printings.

The editor and the publisher make grateful acknowledgments for permission to reprint the following copyright material. Acknowledgments are made by author in alphabetical order.

"A Night of The Full Moon" by Bert Almon from *Calling Texas* (Thistledown Press, 1990), reprinted with permission.

"The Warner Bros./Shakespeare Hour" by Bert Almon from *Deep North*, (Thistledown Press, 1984), reprinted with permission.

"Regarding a Door" by David Antin from *Code of Flag Behaviour* © copyright 1965. Used with permission of David Antin.

"Habitation" from Margaret Atwood's *Selected Poems 1966–1984*, copyright © Margaret Atwood 1990 and "Siren Song" from *Songs of the Transformed*. Reprinted by permission of Oxford University Press Canada.

"Me As My Grandmother" by Rosemary Aubert is reprinted from *Two Kinds of Honey* by permission of Oberon Press.

"The Swimmer's Moment" from *The Sinter Sun and Other Poems* by Margaret Avison. Used by permission of the Canadian Publishers, McClelland & Stewart, Toronto.

"In Westminster Abbey" from *Collected Poems* by John Betjeman. Used by permission of John Murray (Publishers) Ltd.

"Again and Again" from *Last Makings* by Earle Birney. Used by permission of the Canadian Publishers, McClelland & Stewart, Toronto.

"the tomato conspirasee aint worth a whol pome" from *Beyond Even Faithful Legends* by bill bissett, Talonbooks, 1980. Reprinted with permission.

"Graduation Evening" and "The Hoop" by Elizabeth Brewster are reprinted from *The Way Home* by permission of Oberon Press

"Great-Aunt Rebecca" and "New Year's Day, 1978" by Elizabeth Brewster are reprinted from *Selected Poems 1944–1977* by permission of Oberon Press.

"A Moment of Respect" from *I Am A Sensation* by Edwin Brock. Used by permission of the Canadian Publishers, McClelland & Stewart, Toronto.

"Winter Fireflies" by Stephen Brockwell from *Poets 88* reprinted by permission of Quarry Press.

"Marigolds" by Bliss Carman from *Windflowers*, Tecumseh Press, 1985.

"Waiting for the Barbarians" and "Walls" by Constantine P. Cavafy, from *C.P. Cavafy: Selected Poems*, translated by Edmund Keeley and Philip Sherrard. Copyright © 1972 by Princeton University Press. Used by permission of Princeton University Press, U.S.A.

"The Miller's Tale" from *The Canterbury Tales* by Geoffrey Chaucer, translated by Nevill Coghill (Penguin Classics, Rev. ed. 1960) copyright © Nevill Coghill, 1951, 1958, 1960. Used by permission of Penguin Books Ltd., London, England.

"The Elder's Drum" by Molly Chisaakay from *Writing the Circle*, ed. Jeanne Perreault and Sylvia Vance, 1990. Reprinted with permission.

"The Bus" from the book entitled *Flowers for Hitler* by Leonard Cohen, copyright © 1964 Leonard Cohen. Used by Permission. All Rights Reserved.

"Photograph" from *Sometimes All Over* by Don Coles. Used by permission of the author.

"The Streets of Purple Cloth" from *The Small Words In My Body* by Karen Connelly. Used by permission of Kalamalka Press, Vernon, B.C.

242

243

"Ancestral Burden" by Alfonsina Storni from *Anthology of Contemporary Latin-American Poetry*, ed. Dudley Fitts. Copyright © 1942, 1947 by New Directions Publishing Corporation. Reprinted by permission of New Directions Publishing Corporation.

"On Loneliness" by Anne Szumigalski from *Journey/Journée*. Reprinted by permission of Red Deer College Publishing.

"In the Mountains" by Li T'ai-Po reprinted from *A Garden of Peonies*, translated by Henry H. Hart with the permission of the publishers, Stanford University Press. Copyright © 1938 by the Board of Trustees of the Leland Stanford Junior University. Copyright renewed 1966 by Henry S. Hart.

"Post Humus" by Patti Tana from *Ask the Dreamer Where Night Begins*, 1986, found in *When I Am Old I Shall Wear Purple*, Papier-Mache Press, 1987. Reprinted by permission of Kendall Hunt Publishing, Co.

"Praxis" by Sharon Thesen from *Holding the Prose* (Coach House Press, 1983). Reprinted by permission of the author.

"Do Not Go Gentle Into That Good Night" by Dylan Thomas from *The Poems of Dylan Thomas*. J.M. Dent and Sons, Ltd. Reprinted by permission of David Higham Associates.

"The Proposal" by Eva Tihanyi from *Dancing Visions*, Thistledown Press, 1985. Reprinted by permission of Eva Tihanyi.

"Mirror" by John Updike from *The Carpentered Hen and Other Tame Creatures*. Copyright © 1957 by John Updike. Reprinted by Permission of Alfred A. Knopf, Inc.

"Game Called On Account of Darkness" from *Terror and Decorum* by Peter Viereck, 1948. Also published by Greenwood Press (Westport, Conn.) in 1973. Also in *New and Selected Poems* Bobbs-Merrill Co., 1967 and *Archer In The Marrow*, NY Norton, 1987. Used by permission of the author.

"Except for Laura Secord" by Sylvia Maultash Warsh reprinted by permission of the author.

"Crane Lady" by Enos Watts from *Autumn Vengeance*. Published with permission of Breakwater, St.John's, Newfoundland. Copyright Enos Watts.

"Wayman in the Workforce: Actively Seeking Employment" by Tom Wayman from *The Nobel Prize Acceptance Speech*. Copyright 1981. Originally from *Money and Rain*, Macmillan. Reprinted by permission of the author.

"The Mill" by Richard Wilbur from *Things of This World*. Copyright © 1956 and renewed 1984 by Richard Wilbur, reprinted by permission of Harcourt Brace Jovanovich, Inc.

"The Term" by William Carlos Williams from *The Collected Poems of William Carlos Williams, 1909–1939, Vol. I* Copyright © 1938 by New Directions Publishing Corporation. Reprinted by permission of New Directions Publishing Corporation.

"Green River" by Andrew Wreggitt from *Dancing Visions* (Thistledown, 1985) and *South Easterly* (Thistledown, 1987), reprinted with permission.

"Ryokan" by Andrew Wreggitt from *Making Movies*, (Thistledown Press, 1989), reprinted with permission.

"Baptism" by Dale Zieroth from *Mid-River*, The House of Anansi Press. Reprinted by permission of Stoddart Publishing Co., Limited, 34 Lesmill Rd., Don Mills, Ontario, Canada.

FURTHER ACKNOWLEDGMENTS

"Provisions" by Margaret Atwood from *The Animals in That Country*. Copyright © Oxford University Press Canada 1968. Reprinted by permission of Oxford University Press Canada.

"Experience" by Dorothy Livesay reprinted by permission of the author.

"Two Campers in Cloud Country" by Sylvia Plath from *Crossing the Water*. Reprinted by permission of the publishers Faber & Faber Ltd.

246

247

249

UNKNOWN NATIONALITY

USA

251

252

KUBLA KHAN

SAMUEL TAYLOR COLERIDGE

In Xanadu did Kubla Khan
A stately pleasure dome decree:
Where Alph, the sacred river, ran
Through caverns measureless to man
   Down to a sunless sea.
So twice five miles of fertile ground
With walls and towers were girdled round:
And there were gardens bright with sinuous rills,
Where blossomed many an incense-bearing tree;
And here were forests ancient as the hills,
Enfolding sunny spots of greenery.

But oh! that deep romantic chasm which slanted
Down the green hill athwart a cedarn cover!
A savage place! as holy and enchanted
As e'er beneath a waning moon was haunted
By woman wailing for her demon lover!
And from this chasm, with ceaseless turmoil seething,
As if this earth in fast thick pants were breathing,
A mighty fountain momently was forced:
Amid whose swift half-intermitted burst
Huge fragments vaulted like rebounding hail,
Or chaffy grain beneath the thresher's flail:
And 'mid these dancing rocks at once and ever
It flung up momently the sacred river.
Five miles meandering with a mazy motion
Through wood and dale the sacred river ran,
Then reached the caverns measureless to man,

254

And sank in tumult to a lifeless ocean:
And 'mid this tumult Kubla heard from far
Ancestral voices prophesying war!
  The shadow of the dome of pleasure
  Floated midway on the waves:
  Where was heard the mingled measure
  From the fountain and the caves.
It was a miracle of rare device,
A sunny pleasure dome with caves of ice!
  A damsel with a dulcimer
  In a vision once I saw:
  It was an Abyssinian maid,
  And on her dulcimer she played,
  Singing of Mount Abora.
Could I revive within me
Her symphony and song,
To such a deep delight 'twould win me,
That with music loud and long,
I would build that dome in air,
That sunny dome! those caves of ice!
And all who heard should see them there,
And all should cry, Beware! Beware!
His flashing eyes, his floating hair!
Weave a circle round him thrice,
And close your eyes with holy dread,
For he on honeydew hath fed,
And drunk the milk of Paradise.